"This book—full of incr[...] and concise overviews—is hands down the easiest way to understand the hardest book in the Bible: the book of Revelation. This book will enlighten you, spiritually encourage you, and bring many smiles to your face as you read it. Highly recommended!"

Ron Rhodes
Author of *40 Days Through Revelation*

"Todd Hampson, in his follow-up book to *The Non-Prophet's Guide to the End Times*, has done it again. And he has done so with his unique and entertaining flair. He has produced a terrific volume that will stimulate the prophecy student to dig more fervently into biblical eschatology.

The Non-Prophet's Guide to the Book of Revelation moves the reader ever more deeply into the study of prophecy. It is a much-needed volume, a must for anyone concerned about things ahead in the immediate future and beyond."

Terry James
Author, conference speaker
Cohost raptureready.com
Host terryjamesprophecyline.com

"Todd Hampson takes the reader on an unforgettable adventure through Revelation!"

Jeff Kinley
Author, conference speaker

THE NON-PROPHET'S GUIDE TO THE BOOK OF REVELATION

THE NON-PROPHET'S GUIDE™ TO THE BOOK OF REVELATION

Written & Illustrated by
ToDD HAMPSON

HARVEST HOUSE PUBLISHERS
EUGENE, OREGON

Cover design by Kyler Dougherty

Published in association with William K. Jensen Literary Agency, 119 Bampton Court, Eugene, Oregon 97404

The Non-Prophet's Guide™ to the Book of Revelation
Copyright © 2019—text © by Todd Hampson; artwork © by Todd Hampson
Published by Harvest House Publishers
Eugene, Oregon 97408
www.harvesthousepublishers.com

ISBN 978-0-7369-7540-7 (pbk)
ISBN 978-0-7369-7541-4 (eBook)

Library of Congress Cataloging-in-Publication Data

Names: Hampson, Todd, author.
Title: The non-prophet's guide to the Book of Revelation / Todd Hampson.
Description: Eugene : Harvest House Publishers, 2019. | Includes
    bibliographical references.
Identifiers: LCCN 2019005720 (print) | LCCN 2019019876 (ebook) | ISBN
    9780736975414 (ebook) | ISBN 9780736975407 (pbk.)
Subjects: LCSH: Bible. Revelation--Criticism, interpretation, etc.
Classification: LCC BS2825.52 (ebook) | LCC BS2825.52 .H34 2019 (print) | DDC
    228/.06--dc23
LC record available at https://lccn.loc.gov/2019005720

Printed in the United States of America

21 22 23 24 25 26 27 / VP-CD / 10 9 8 7 6 5

Dedicated to my dad, Richard Hampson.
Your entrepreneurial spirit, work ethic,
kindness, humility, and quiet strength
have led and equipped me more than you realize.
And your encouraging support over the years
has blessed me and my family in tremendous ways.
With love and admiration, Todd.

CONTENTS

INTRODUCTION

An Unexpected Adventure

Blessed is the one who reads aloud the words of this prophecy, and blessed are those who hear it and take to heart what is written in it, because the time is near.

REVELATION 1:3

As you sit on the edge of the boat with one hand on your mask and regulator and the other on the back of your head, thoughts race through your mind. You consider how far from land you are, and you wonder if the handful of sharks you just watched eating their chum a few feet away from the small charter boat are still hungry. Fear and excitement swell as you cross your legs and lean back to let gravity do the rest. Three, two, one, drop!

Splash! The cool Caribbean water engulfs you as the noise of seagulls suddenly changes to the sound of bubbles and Darth Vader-like breathing as you force air through the regulator into your lungs. You are now in the Atlantic Ocean—an hour away from land and surrounded by otherworldly sea life. Recalling your recent training, you stabilize your ears and slowly descend the diving reel to the sunken ship on the ocean floor 50 feet below.

As you descend, you take note of the cloudy spot of leftover chum above and the silhouettes of a few Caribbean reef shark hoping for more. About 20 feet further down, you come face to face with a large, ugly fish—a giant grouper—hovering in place and unintimidated by your presence. Off in the distance you spot the complete darkness of the 6,000-feet underwater cliff known as the Tongue of the Ocean—a branch of the Great Bahama Canyon. A healthy fear is present, along with a rush of adrenaline, as your thoughts turn to the amazing beauty of the coral reefs and schools of bright-colored fish below. Words can't adequately describe the scene. Heightening the experience is the realization that just four hours ago, this adventure of a lifetime was not even on the agenda.

TONGUE OF THE OCEAN AKA TOTO

DEEP-OCEAN U-SHAPED TRENCH
NEAR THE BAHAMAS
20 MILES WIDE, 150 MILES LONG
DROPS FROM 70 FEET TO 6000+ FEET
PART OF THE GREAT BAHAMA CANYON

That was the experience my wife and I had on the last full day of our honeymoon in the Bahamas. We traveled to an all-inclusive resort featuring great dining and various activities you could enjoy without ever leaving the resort. We took a kayak to an island one day, went water skiing another, and enjoyed relaxing on the beach on yet another. Toward the end of our stay we met with the concierge to inquire about other activities, and they called our attention to the daily scuba diving excursions.

QUICK FACT: DID YOU KNOW...
that SCUBA stands for Self-Contained Underwater Breathing Apparatus?

We were surprised to learn we could take a two-hour class on site, then pass a quick scuba and swimming test to be dive-certified in the Bahamas. The timing was perfect—a class was just about to start, and we discovered that there was still room on a scuba excursion that was set to leave soon after the training. Within a short period of time our day transitioned from a fairly routine vacation morning to one of the most memorable adventures of our lives.

Your Next Adventure Revealed

Think about an unexpected adventure you have had. Some of the best experiences in life come when we don't expect them. Many Christians in our day don't realize that studying the book of Revelation is just such an adventure! Though the last book of the Bible is often seen as scary, complicated, irrelevant, divisive, confusing, or boring, the truth is that studying Revelation with the right perspective is one of the most practical, relevant, and exciting things you can do as a believer in Christ! Unfortunately, the enemy has convinced many that reading Revelation isn't worth the time—because he knows that his destruction, our ultimate redemption, and the Lord's glorification are all detailed in this breathtaking capstone of the Bible!

You are about to embark on a thrilling trek that will cause your faith in the Bible, and your excitement about the nearness of the Lord's return, to bloom with new meaning. If you long for hope, joy, clarity, and a majestic sense of your calling, you need to study the phenomenal truths awaiting you in the book of Revelation.

When it comes to everything that is happening in today's world, God's hand is still on the steering wheel. Nothing is random or accidental. Everything is falling into place exactly as God foretold. Christ's return has been nearly 2,000 years in the making, and we are on the cusp of the most astounding supernatural events of Scripture—a season that prophecy experts such as the late Chuck Missler have said the Bible talks more about than any other period of history. If you want a clear picture about what is soon to take place, get ready for your adventure!

What We'll Discover

Together on this journey, we'll see a full picture of Jesus reigning in power and glory. We'll learn what the often-overlooked letters to the churches (Revelation chapters 2–3) mean for us today. We'll uncover the fascinating details about the rapture. We'll understand—perhaps for the first time—that the book of Revelation is to be taken literally and that the symbols are meant to be understood. We'll study the various judgments, as well as the technology, culture, and current events that demonstrate we are rapidly approaching the last days—and that we are nearer than ever to the rapture of the church!

We'll discover the long-suffering patience of God as he delays his judgment as far as his holiness will allow. We'll learn how even God's wrath is designed to bring the maximum number of people into heaven. We'll see how Revelation ties up every major theme introduced in Genesis. We'll come to understand God's purpose and plan for Israel and the Jewish people. And we'll unpack key details about the glorious future that awaits us in the millennial kingdom and the eternal state!

Revelation is the climax of God's Word, the crescendo of his redemptive plan, the magnum opus of his message. It unveils the ultimate resolution of all things. So buckle up and get ready to study one of the most thrilling—and most overlooked—books of the Bible. This is one unexpected adventure you don't want to miss. Let's dive in!

CHAPTER 1

One Mega-Story

Do not think that I have come to abolish the Law or the Prophets; I have not come to abolish them but to fulfill them. For truly I tell you, until heaven and earth disappear, not the smallest letter, not the least stroke of a pen, will by any means disappear from the Law until everything is accomplished.

MATTHEW 5:17-18

One of my favorite college courses was a radio, television, and film class called "The Analysis and Structure of Film." Throughout the course we would watch and analyze classic films, then write a detailed report about a particular shot or sequence. One point our professor made abundantly clear was this: Nothing that appears on the screen is there by accident. Not a single detail in a shot or sequence is random. Every nuance has a purpose and was intentionally placed there by the director to achieve his overall vision for the film. Our instructor demonstrated how the shot sequences, camera angles, lighting, colors, composition, movement, patterns, editing rhythm, and every other controllable detail in a good film serves to support the story and the director's vision.

On a much deeper level, I believe the same is true when it comes to Scripture. If we zoom in to a specific story in Scripture, it holds up on its own as a complete story. When we pull back to view the broader context—like a chapter or a complete book—we see it fits into a larger story. If we pull back to reveal the full context, we see that the entire Bible is cohesively designed into one grand mega-story. Nowhere is this more evident than in Scripture's final book, which brings resolution to every key theme of the Bible.

39 WRITERS
3 CONTINENTS
1500 YEARS
1 STORY

God is the author who inspired the Bible's writers, and every minute detail is intentional—without an inkling of randomness. The very structure of Scripture, the nuances of the Hebrew and Greek and Aramaic languages, the typology, the numerology, the specific details of prophecies and their fulfillments—and so many other details—demonstrate God's clear handiwork. It's as if the Bible itself has a divine DNA that runs through it from Genesis to Revelation. The more you study the Scriptures, the more evident this truth becomes.

2 Peter 1:20-21—Above all, you must understand that no prophecy of Scripture came about by the prophet's own interpretation of things. For prophecy never had its origin in the human will, but prophets, though human, spoke from God as they were carried along by the Holy Spirit.

The Critical Link: Origins and Last Things

Each divine DNA strand begins its journey in Genesis and finds its ultimate resolution in Revelation. No two books have been attacked or neglected more than these two bookends of Scripture. Naturalists and liberal theologians have sought to undermine the authenticity and reliability of Genesis for the past 250 years. The enemy would like nothing more than to divert our attention away from the essential truths found there. If this critical foundation is cracked (at least in the hearts and minds of people), the rest of the structure is likely to be misunderstood or even ignored.

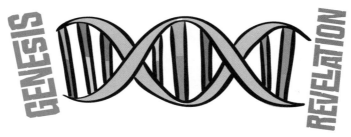

On the other end of the biblical spectrum, the book of Revelation is often seen as confusing at best and utterly unknowable or irrelevant at worst. We shouldn't be surprised that both Genesis and Revelation are under attack these days—just as we are nearing the end of the age.

John 10:10—The thief comes only to steal and kill and destroy; I have come that they may have life, and have it to the full.

There is a critical link between these two key books, and the enemy has done his best to keep us disinterested or preoccupied so we miss the all-important truths found within them. In Genesis we discover our roots, and in Revelation we learn about our eternal future. Every key theme and theological truth finds its origin in Genesis and its ultimate culmination in Revelation. The Bible is a "book of books" that begins with eternity past and ends with eternity future. The core questions that people have about their origins and their future are answered by these two critical books—meticulously woven together by the other 64 books between them.

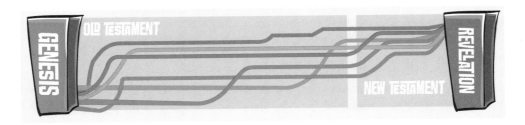

Rediscovering the Old Testament

John assumed his readers would be familiar with the Old Testament. In fact, Revelation is a distinctly Jewish book. In it we find all kinds of Jewish symbolism, two Jewish witnesses, 144,000 Jewish evangelists, and the world's attention centered on Israel and Jerusalem during the end times. In Revelation's 404 verses there are more than 800 references or allusions to the Old Testament![1]

The symbolism in Revelation is solved either by reading the immediate context in which it appears or by cross-referencing passages from the Old Testament. Many Bible expositors teach what is known as "the law of first mention." To understand the doctrines or symbols used in Revelation, you must find the first place in Scripture that doctrine or symbol is mentioned. The first instance of a teaching or symbol in Scripture often provides tremendous insight into how it is to be understood later. Cross-referencing all the uses of a key word or term will help you to build upon the doctrine or symbol's first mention.

This approach helps us interpret Scripture with Scripture, instead of interpreting Scripture based on outside sources or our own thoughts and ideas. If God is the author of the Bible, we should expect to find a cohesiveness in this regard—and we do. The law of first mention, and the principle of interpreting scripture with scripture, both bear out a divine unity in God's Word as it relates to numbers, symbols, doctrines, names, places, and many other details. Using the law of first mention—and interpreting scripture with scripture—when studying Revelation helps to bring great clarity to most of the symbolism found in the book.

QUICK FACT: DID YOU KNOW...

the number 7 is a big deal in Revelation? The first mention of 7 is in the creation account in Genesis. This number speaks of completeness, fullness, or rest.

Daniel: The Revelation of the Old Testament

While all the Old Testament prophets provide important details about end-time events, the book that provides the most sweeping view—and that, in some ways, serves as a foundation for Revelation—is Daniel. Sometimes

Daniel is referred to as the "Revelation of the Old Testament," which is why seminary level-courses designed to study Revelation often look at the book of Daniel as well.

Eight of the twelve chapters in Daniel center on prophecy. Having a basic understanding of this prophetic two-thirds of Daniel sheds much light on world history and the end times. In Daniel 2, we read a sweeping (and amazingly accurate) prophecy about a statue that represents four successive world kingdoms (Babylon, Medo-Persia, Greece, Rome) that would precede a loosely united end-time kingdom in the last days. In Daniel 7, we see these same kingdoms depicted as four beasts, followed by an end-time revived kingdom out of which will emerge an end-time evil ruler (seen as a little horn).

In Daniel 8, we see a more detailed view of Medo-Persia and Greece—particularly the conquests of Alexander the Great and the dividing of the Greek Empire (prophesied more than two centuries before the events took place). Chapter 8 ends with some key details about the evil end-times ruler.

THE KINGDOMS

GOD SILVER BRONZE IRON IRON/CLAY

BABYLON
612 BC

MEDO-PERSIA
539 BC

GREECE
330 BC

ROME
63 BC

REVIVED ROME
END-TIMES
CONFIGURATION

DANIEL 2   DANIEL 7

In chapter 9 we learn about a 490-year period that provides the timing of the first coming of Christ, a mysterious gap period (that we now know as the church age—the period we currently find ourselves in), and a final seven-year period during which an evil ruler will come to power. The last four verses of Daniel 9 are arguably the most important verses of the entire book. These four short verses contain an incredible prophecy that covers all of Jewish history from Daniel's time to the end.

THE 70 WEEKS OF DANIEL CHAPTER 9

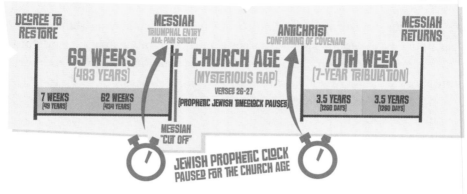

This final seven-year span mentioned in the Daniel 9 prophecy is known to us as the tribulation. This seven-year period is detailed in the book of Revelation and makes up most of its content (Revelation 6:1–19:21).

VARIOUS NAMES USED FOR
THE TRIBULATION PERIOD

Jacob's trouble	(Jeremiah 30:7)
Daniel's 70th week	(Daniel 9:24-27)
A time of distress	(Daniel 12:1)
The great day	(Revelation 6:17)
The hour of testing	(Revelation 3:10)
The indignation	(Isaiah 26:20)
Tribulation/Great Tribulation	(Matthew 24:9, 21, 29; Mark 13:19, 24; Rev. 7:14)
The Day of the Lord	(Joel 1:15; 2:1; 1 Thess. 5:2)

In Daniel 11 we find further details about the future (from Daniels' perspective) Greek Empire; then beginning in verse 36 the prophecy shifts to the evil end-time ruler. Daniel 11:36-45 provides several facts about this ruler and the events that will take place during his reign. Chapter 12 continues this description and gives us information about the last three-and-a-half years of the seven-year tribulation period.

A careful study of the visions of Daniel (particularly chapters 2, 7, 8, 9, 11, and 12) lays the foundation for studying Revelation. Daniel serves as a sort of blueprint or grid through which we can better understand Revelation. As you read through the prophetic passages in Daniel, much light will be shed on the events, timing, and symbolism of Revelation.

Is Revelation Practical?

This is a relevant question. With all the struggles people go through in life, and with all the significant physical needs and global crises present in our world today, why should we take the time to study Revelation with all of its symbolism, mysteries, apocalyptic language, and scary scenarios?

Because it's the capstone of Scripture, the climax of the story, the resolution of the biblical narrative. Ignoring Revelation would be like going to a movie and walking out before the best part!

In practical terms, understanding Revelation gives us a deeper confidence in Scripture, anchors our focus on a promised future and eternal hope, purifies our Christian life, pushes us to share our faith, and helps us make sense of the way the world is today.

As we embark on this incredibly practical overview of the most amazing—yet most avoided—book of the Bible, keep your knowledge of the Old Testament running in the background. I'll include relevant cross-references when needed to help clarify various passages of Revelation. You're in for a treat as we jump into Revelation 1, where you will see a new and radical picture of the risen and reigning Jesus.

CHAPTER 2

The Full Picture of Jesus—Meek and Wild

The Revelation of Jesus Christ, which God gave Him to show His servants—things which must shortly take place. And He sent and signified it by His angel to His servant John.

REVELATION 1:1 (NKJV)

In the art world, there's a technique known as single-point perspective. When drawing a scene or background, this method offers a simple way to add the illusion of depth for a two-dimensional composition. Key to this concept is a single point on the horizon known to artists as the vanishing point. This is the point where all perspective lines converge, giving the illusion of infinite distance. Once the vanishing point is established, straight guidelines are drawn from the edges of the page to the vanishing point. These guidelines are then used to render the composition with the illusion of depth—portraying three-dimensional space on a two-dimensional surface.

Once the vanishing point and guidelines are erased, covered, or turned off (for digitally created art), the composed scene has a sense of cohesion and depth. The casual observer won't notice the vanishing point or the perspective guidelines,

but the trained artist can spot the location of the vanishing point by studying the details of the composition. This all-important invisible anchor ties the entire piece of art together.

The Bible has such an anchor that everything else in Scripture is tethered to—the person of Jesus Christ. The opening verse of the final book in God's Word zeroes in on this paramount fact. The capstone book of Scripture is all about the revelation—or the unveiling—of the Lord Jesus Christ in all his fullness! Every storyline, theological trail, theme, and prophetic marker points to Jesus like guidelines directing our eyes to the vanishing point of a priceless piece of art. The opening verse and the initial vision of the glorified Christ in Revelation 1 affirms this fact, as do many other scriptures.

> Luke 24:27—Beginning with Moses and all the Prophets, he explained to them what was said in **ALL** the Scriptures concerning himself (emphasis added).

In Genesis 3:15, we discover the first prophecy pointing to the Savior, then in Revelation we find him finishing his work and reigning as King of kings and Lord of lords. The pages between Genesis and Revelation connect all the key scriptural themes to Jesus—the anchor point of the biblical narrative.

> Genesis 3:15—I will put enmity between you and the woman, and between your offspring and hers; he will crush your head, and you will strike his heel.

The last book of the Bible opens with a revelation of Jesus and crescendos with John's stunning vision of the glorified Christ. So that we can appreciate this more, let's look at some important details in the buildup to John's incredible vision.

Details, Details, Details

Often we view the first few verses of a book of the Bible as fluff or generic set-up material—much like we view the opening to a modern-day letter: "To Whom It May Concern, blah blah blah…"—okay, let's get to the good stuff! When we make this assumption with Scripture, however, we miss important preliminary details—especially here in the book of Revelation. The very first verse of chapter 1 (provided at the opening of this chapter) contains critical foundational information that is easy to overlook.

We learn from this opening verse how the message of the book was transmitted. It came directly from the Father, was given to the Son, who then gave the message to an angel, who was to give it to John so he could record it for us—his servants. It's like a divine game of telephone—except we have received the information accurately! Nothing was lost in transmission from God's heart to his people.

THE NON-PROPHET PLAYS "TELEPHONE"

…AND HE SENT AND SIGNIFIED IT BY HIS ANGEL TO HIS SERVANT JOHN.

OHHH…KAYY…

ANDY SENT SAND DIGNIFIED BY DEANGELO TO SURF'S-UP JOHN!

Unsealed Truth

In the Old Testament, Daniel was told that some of the prophecies he was given were to be sealed or hidden until the time of the end. Daniel saw some amazing visions about the tribulation that he didn't understand. He wanted to know more but was told in Daniel 12:9 that the "words are rolled up and sealed until the time of the end."

By contrast, we find here in the opening verse of Revelation that God will unseal the prophecies about end-time events. This is the *revelation* or the *apocalypse* (from the Greek word translated "unveiling") from Jesus Christ.

In Hebrews 1:1-2 we learn that the "last days" have already begun. There we read, "In the past God spoke to our ancestors through the prophets at many times and in various ways, *but in these last days* he has spoken to us by his Son, whom he appointed heir of all things, and through whom also he made the universe" (emphasis added).

This tells us we're in the last days or the last time period—what is commonly known as the age of grace or the church age, which began at Pentecost (Acts 2). God unveiled details regarding the end times and the return of Christ as a key focus for the church age. What was hidden from Daniel has now been revealed for those living in the church age—that includes us! No story is complete without an ending. Revelation offers us unsealed insight into the resolution of all things. It finishes the redemptive narrative that began in Genesis.

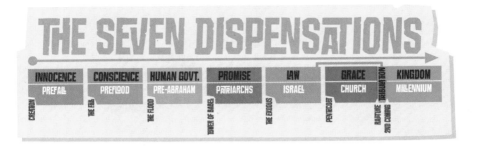

The End-Time Tachometer

One term that often trips people up when they read the opening verse of Revelation is the word *shortly*. The verse tells us that the things described in the book of Revelation "must shortly take place"—but it's been nearly 2,000 years since John wrote those words. We understand from 2 Peter 3:8 that for God, 1,000 years is as a day, but is there more clarifying information here to consider? Yes!

2 Peter 3:8—Do not forget this one thing, dear friends: With the Lord a day is like a thousand years, and a thousand years are like a day.

The Greek word used here is *tachos*, which forms the base of the English word *tachometer*. It refers to the speed at which events occur once they start, not the closeness or proximity of an event. In other words, the end-time events—once they start—will take place in rapid succession.

ta•chom•e•ter = an instrument that
noun   measures speed of rotation

The bulk of Revelation describes the events that will take place during the seven-year tribulation period. Once set in motion by the rapture and the enforcing of a seven-year agreement by the antichrist, all the judgments described in Revelation will occur in increasingly rapid succession.

tach•os (takh'-os) = swiftness,
noun   speed, hastily

Signs and Symbols

Yet another key—and easily overlooked—word in the opening verse of Revelation has to do with the symbols we find in the book. We are told that God "signified" (NKJV) the message through the angel to give to John. He conveyed the message by signs or symbols. When we observe wordless road signs or various international symbols, we understand what they mean by their simplicity and context. With this key word *signified* we are given a clue as to the main literary device that would be used in Revelation.

se•ma•i•no (say-mah'-ee-no) =
Greek   to make known by a sign

This does not mean that the symbols are to be spiritualized and thus lose their meaning. Rather, it means that the symbols point to a greater reality—a fulfillment of that symbol's typology from the Old Testament. It's as if someone condensed all the themes from the Old Testament and poured them into Revelation, where we find their ultimate fulfillment. Whenever a symbol is used in Revelation, we must do a bit of homework to see how this symbol was used elsewhere in Scripture. We don't get to pick and decide for ourselves the meaning of the symbols. We should allow the Bible to reveal their meanings as we track down the symbols' previous uses in Scripture. As I mentioned in the previous chapter, the larger context of God's Word helps to provide the meaning of each specific symbol. We should let Scripture interpret Scripture whenever symbols are used.

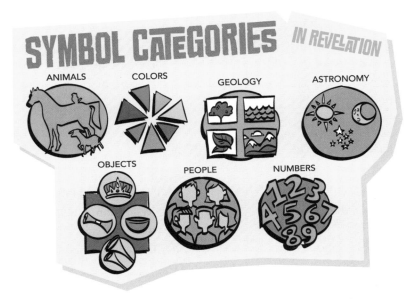

An Astounding Promise

At the outset of this amazing book is a promise unlike any other in Scripture. In Revelation 1:3 we read, "Blessed is the one who reads aloud the words of this prophecy, and blessed are those who hear it and take to heart what is written in it, because the time is near."

As far as I know, this is the only book of the Bible that makes the promise that whoever reads it will be blessed! Isn't it ironic that Revelation is also one of the most neglected books of the Bible? It's clear why the enemy has done so much to turn our eyes away from this book. I can say from firsthand experience that as a result of studying Revelation, I have a much deeper understanding of Scripture, a greater confidence that every original word of the Bible is divinely inspired, a keener understanding of our times, and a more passionate expectation of the Lord's return. These blessings come directly from reading Revelation, and they influence my daily walk with the Lord in profound and practical ways.

Verses 4-8 contain a wealth of additional set-up information for Revelation. Whole sermons could be preached on each verse. Because this book is an overview of Revelation and not a verse-by-verse in-depth study, I won't cover these verses here, but I recommend you pause for a moment and read them slowly and prayerfully. The rich depth of what they say undergirds the rest of the book, so it's worthwhile to take the time to study and ponder them for yourself. Notice here the identity of the audience—the seven churches in Asia Minor (modern-day Turkey). In the next chapter we'll look at Christ's words to these churches and the immediate and prophetic applications of those words.

The Setting

Verse 9 of Revelation 1 gives us the setting of the book. John wrote, "I, John, your brother and companion in the suffering and kingdom and patient endurance that are ours in Jesus, was on the island of Patmos because of the word of God and the testimony of Jesus." Extrabiblical (outside of the Bible) sources also confirm that John was exiled to Patmos by the Roman emperor Domitian for preaching the gospel. We also understand from extrabiblical sources that John returned from his exile after the emperor died. Domitian died in AD 96, so traditionally the writing of Revelation has been dated to around AD 90–95.[1]

The apostle John wrote five books of the New Testament, including Revelation. John was a Galilean fisherman—he was born in Bethsaida to a

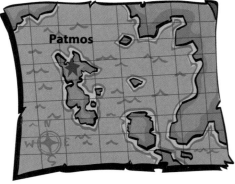

father named Zebedee and a mother named Salome. John and his brother, James, were early disciples of John the Baptist.

Most importantly, in terms of Jesus's ministry, John was one of the inner circle of three (Peter, James, and John) who witnessed the transfiguration (Matthew 17:1-13). He was also self-described in the book of John as "the one whom Jesus loved" (John 13:23; 19:26; 21:7).

In other words, in human terms, John was close to Jesus. He was the only disciple who remained at the cross when all the others abandoned Jesus. John was also given the task of caring for Jesus's mother, Mary, even though Jesus had earthly siblings (Matthew 13:55-56; Mark 6:3).

> John 19:26-27—When Jesus saw his mother there, and the disciple whom he loved standing nearby, he said to her, "Woman, here is your son," and to the disciple, "Here is your mother." From that time on, this disciple took her into his home.

The Day of the Lord

Another interesting detail related to the setting John described when he received the visions of Revelation is found in verse 10, where John wrote, "On the Lord's Day I was in the Spirit, and I heard behind me a loud voice like a trumpet." The literal translation of this would be rendered, "I was in the spirit on the Day of the Lord." In the Old Testament, the phrase "the Day of the Lord" is used to refer to the tribulation period. It's possible John may have been referring to the Lord's day, or Sunday, but many Bible scholars say John was indicating that the Lord had taken him into the spirit realm to witness key events of the tribulation.

OLD AND NEW TESTAMENT REFERENCES TO THE DAY OF THE LORD

OLD TESTAMENT

Isaiah 2:12; 13:6, 9
Ezekiel 13:5; 30:3
Joel 1:15; 2:1, 11, 31; 3:14
Amos 5:18, 20
Obadiah 15
Zephaniah 1:7, 14
Zechariah 14:1
Malachi 4:5

NEW TESTAMENT

Acts 2:20
1 Corinthians 5:5
2 Corinthians 1:14
1 Thessalonians 5:2
2 Thessalonians 2:2
2 Peter 3:10
Revelation 6:17; 16:14

Jesus Unveiled

And now, the big reveal of Revelation chapter 1. If this chapter were a movie, verses 12-18 would be the epic and unexpected scene that has audiences talking. This opening chapter of Revelation—full of critical set-up details—peaks with some mind-blowing specifics from John's vision of the glorified Christ.

We read the following in Revelation 1:12-18:

> I turned around to see the voice that was speaking to me. And when I turned I saw seven golden lampstands, and among the lampstands was someone *like* a son of man, dressed in a robe reaching down to his feet and with a golden sash around his chest. The hair on his head was white *like* wool, as white as snow, and his eyes were *like* blazing fire. His feet were *like* bronze glowing in a furnace, and his voice was

like the sound of rushing waters. In his right hand he held seven stars, and coming out of his mouth was a sharp, double-edged sword. His face was *like* the sun shining in all its brilliance.

When I saw him, I fell at his feet as though dead. Then he placed his right hand on me and said: "Do not be afraid. I am the First and the Last. I am the Living One; I was dead, and now look, I am alive for ever and ever! And I hold the keys of death and Hades" (emphasis mine).

Did you notice how many times John uses the word "like"? The details about the risen and now-glorified Savior were so otherworldly that John had to use descriptive terms his readers would be familiar with—like pure snow, blazing fire, bronze glowing in a fire, the sound of rushing water. But none of these adequately describe what John saw. I've been on a few missions trips, and upon returning home, I've found that trying to describe my experiences to others is difficult. Words cannot convey how my life was affected. John experienced this phenomenon—on steroids.

We're all familiar with the first-coming version of Jesus—the baby born in Bethlehem, the 12-year-old boy in the temple courts, the one who healed the sick and performed miracles, the "meek and mild" Jesus who quietly accepted all the abuse heaped on him as he laid down his life for us at the cross. Revelation reminds us that these snapshots tell only part of the story. Jesus came the first time as a suffering servant. At his return in Revelation 19, he will be seen in all his glory—coming as a warrior-king to settle all accounts and take his rightful place as sovereign of the universe. We see this in full stunning view when Jesus returns at the end of the tribulation—piercing the darkness with bright glory, coming to the world as a horse-riding warrior wearing a bloody robe and with a sword coming out of his mouth as he leads the armies of heaven.

Revelation 19:11-13—I saw heaven standing open and there before me was a white horse, whose rider is called Faithful and True. With justice he judges and wages war. His eyes are like blazing fire, and on his head are many crowns. He has a name written on him that no one knows but he himself. He is dressed in a robe dipped in blood, and his name is the Word of God.

I mentioned earlier in this chapter that the purpose of Revelation is to give us a full picture of Jesus. To get this full picture, we must know how it all ends. Revelation peels back the curtain to show us what is to come and how it all points to Christ. Revelation 19:10 even states, "It is the Spirit of prophecy who bears testimony to Jesus." In other words, the Holy Spirit, who inspired all of Scripture, put prophecy in the Bible specifically to point us to the truth about who Jesus is!

The Outline

Another critical detail given in the opening chapter of Revelation is the outline of the book. In verse 19 we read, "Write, therefore, what you have seen, what is now and what will take place later." The basic outline of Revelation, then, is provided for us by Jesus himself. This is very helpful in terms of understanding the book. This fact shows us that the bulk of the book was future prophecy and that there is an intentional structure to Revelation. We are meant to understand it as future prophecy related to the end times.

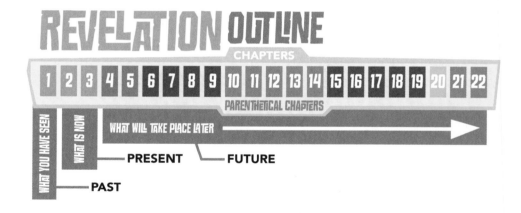

So What?

Why is it so important to have a complete picture of Jesus? Because it changes everything. As we struggle to understand why evil is allowed to flourish and a thousand other similar questions, we see here that God is still in complete control. Jesus is in his rightful place, and there is an appointed time set for him to settle all accounts and make everything right. The thin veil that separates our world and the unseen world will come crashing in, and our faith will become sight as we behold the fiery-eyed, gloriously glowing, and unstoppable Jesus! Let that be the backdrop as we journey through the book of Revelation together.

Let's start by taking a look at the seven hidden epistles of the New Testament—John's letters to the seven churches.

CHAPTER 3

Seven Overlooked Letters Written to You

To the seven churches in the province of Asia:
Grace and peace to you from him who
is, and who was, and who is to come.

REVELATION 1:4

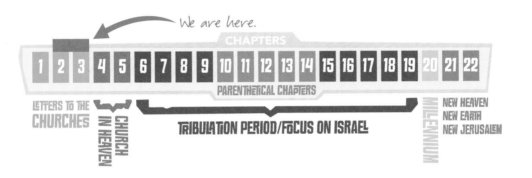

We are here.

CHAPTERS

1 2 3 4 5 6 7 8 9 10 11 12 13 14 15 16 17 18 19 20 21 22

PARENTHETICAL CHAPTERS

LETTERS TO THE CHURCHES | CHURCH IN HEAVEN | TRIBULATION PERIOD/FOCUS ON ISRAEL | MILLENNIUM | NEW HEAVEN NEW EARTH NEW JERUSALEM

The young shepherd climbed his way up the barren limestone cliff. The desert sun beat down on him, causing sweat to roll down his forehead and collect in his eyebrows. He was used to the dry heat, but climbing the rough terrain during the hottest part of the day wasn't part of his plan. His adrenaline sharpened his focus as he looked for natural footholds in the cliff wall. Frustration grew as he pursued the stray that was causing this unplanned excursion away from his flock of sheep and goats.

After navigating the rugged desert terrain for a few minutes, he noticed something he had never seen before in the crevice of a steep hill. The brilliant sunlight on the light-colored soil stood in stark contrast to what appeared to be a dark cave entrance. Curiosity overwhelmed him, so he climbed toward it. When he was close enough to confirm it was indeed a cave, he found a rock and threw it into the center of the shadowy blackness.

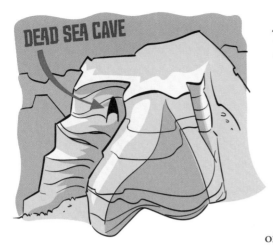

DEAD SEA CAVE

The young shepherd awaited the echo of the stone bouncing off the cave's interior walls, hoping to get an idea of its depth. Before abandoning his rescue mission, he wanted to find out whether this unexpected adventure was worth the treacherous climb he had endured. The earthen projectile that his hand had hurled sent back an unanticipated surprise. Instead of the familiar sound of stone on stone, the shepherd heard the distinct noise of clay pottery breaking.

Forgetting the sweat in his eyes and the burning in his quads, the shepherd scrambled up the hill. As he moved in haste, his sandals filled up with loose dirt and small limestone pebbles. Upon arriving at the mouth of the cave, he shook the debris out of his footwear. He then peered in but was unable to see very far. As his eyes adjusted to the darkness, he carefully moved forward, but the cave seemed empty. Just as he was about to turn around and leave, he spotted the unintended target of the rock he had thrown. It had shattered a large clay jar—one of a collection of several ancient sealed jars that rested on the cave floor.

This account may read like the beginning of an Indiana Jones movie, but this amazing discovery took place in 1947, and the story is that of a young Bedouin shepherd. The hidden treasure was found near the Dead Sea, east of Jerusalem, where the topography suddenly drops three-fourths of a mile to the lowest point on the earth's surface. This barren desert, full of rich biblical history—including Jesus's temptations, David's flight from Saul, and other key events of Scripture—had served as the hiding place for the Dead Sea Scrolls for about 2,000 years.

The shepherd's accidental find was of one of the greatest archeological discoveries of the twentieth century and led to the eventual uncovering of 12 caves full of hundreds of hidden scrolls that were sealed in clay pots like the one broken by the shepherd's rock. These artifacts had been hidden by members of the ancient Qumran community who lived in the area from about 143 BC to AD 68, when the center was destroyed by Roman legions. In the decades since the initial discovery, 11 more caves have been found and a total of 972 manuscripts have been catalogued—pieced together from thousands of pieces of ancient scrolls.

What we now refer to as the Dead Sea Scrolls detailed life in the ancient Qumran community and gave scholars full copies or portions of every Old Testament book except for Nehemiah and Esther. These newfound scrolls were more than 1,000 years older than any other Old Testament manuscript in existence. As a matter of providence,

they were discovered the same year that Resolution 181 was passed by the United Nations. This resolution called for the land known as Palestine to be divided into Arab and Jewish states, and directly set the stage for Israel's prophesied rebirth in 1948. Many people believe the Lord kept the scrolls hidden "in plain sight" for 2,000 years until it was time for Israel's rebirth. The Dead Sea Scrolls proved Israel's claim to the region as her ancient homeland, and the discovery of these documents served as a timely precursor to the nation's rebirth.

For 2,000 years, the Dead Sea scrolls were overlooked. This rich discovery awaited the right time and a curious explorer. By analogy, I would say that Revelation chapters 2 and 3 are treasures hidden in plain sight—treasures that await similar explorers. Rich practical insights that are relevant to our times and the life of every believer lay undiscovered or overlooked by many Christians today.

In their eagerness to get to the dramatic events beginning in Revelation chapter 4, many people tend to skip over or breeze through chapters 2–3. If you think about it, these chapters contain seven additional epistles (or letters) of the New Testament—letters that are embedded in the larger work of Revelation. They are short letters, but so are Philemon, 2 John, 3 John, and Jude. These four epistles consist of only 13-25 verses each, yet they contain important truths God wants us to know.

Introduction to the Letters

The immediate audience of John's book were the seven churches of Asia Minor, all of which were located in what is now Turkey. These churches existed during the time of the Roman Empire, and their archeological remains have been uncovered and documented. These seven churches in the cities of Ephesus, Smyrna, Pergamum, Thyatira, Sardis, Philadelphia, and Laodicea. This raises a question: The book of Acts and other New Testament letters feature some additional prominent churches, so why did John pick these seven? They were probably churches that John oversaw prior to his exile. There are also prophetic reasons for choosing these seven churches—reasons that are detailed below.

 **...IS REALLY IMPORTANT IN THE BIBLE,** and especially in Bible prophecy! As you read various prophecies, notice how many times the number 7 comes up! It is the number of fullness or completion, and we find its first use in the 6 days of creation and the seventh day for rest, which gave us our 7-day week.

Letter Structure

The seven letters each follow a similar structure, which includes a title or description of Jesus, a commendation, a correction, an instruction, and a reward. There are a few telling deviations from this structure. For example, the Lord had nothing negative to say about the churches in Smyrna and Philadelphia (the persecuted church and the missionary church), and he had nothing good to say about the churches in Sardis and Laodicea (the denominational and lukewarm churches).

I encourage you to pause here and read each of the seven letters to the churches in Revelation chapters 2–3 so you can familiarize yourself with them prior to reading the rest of this chapter.

Each letter is addressed to "the angel" of the designated church. Some Bible experts believe that the term "angel" could refer to a guardian or an overseeing angel for each of these churches. But a more thorough study of Scripture better supports the idea that Jesus is addressing the pastors of those churches. The original Greek word translated "angel" simply means "messenger," and nowhere else in Scripture is man seen giving a message to an angel. In fact, it's always the other way around when a divine message is delivered and angels are involved.

GO AHEAD. I'LL HOLD DOWN THE FORT UNTIL YOU GET BACK.

A full chapter could be written about the historical background of each church along with a phrase-by-phrase breakdown of Jesus's letter to each church, but for the purposes of this overview, I've provided this chart so you can quickly see the key features of each letter.

INSTRUCTIONS FROM JESUS TO THE 7 CHURCHES

	DESCRIPTION	COMMENDATION	REPROOF	INSTRUCTION	REWARD
EPHESUS	HOLDS 7 STARS, WALKS AMONG THE LAMPSTANDS (i.e., churches)	RECOGNIZES THEIR HARD WORK/DEEDS AND DOCTRINE	LEFT THEIR FIRST LOVE	DO WHAT YOU DID BEFORE	EAT FROM TREE OF LIFE
SMYRNA	FIRST AND LAST, DIED AND ROSE AGAIN	RICH IN FAITH PERSEVERE THROUGH PERSECUTION	NONE	STAY FAITHFUL EVEN TO DEATH	VICTOR'S CROWN AND ETERNAL LIFE
PERGAMUM	HIM WHO HAS SHARP 2-SIDED SWORD	HELD ONTO FAITH DESPITE PERSECUTION	TOLERATED OCCULT TEACHING AND IMMORALITY	REPENT OR **JESUS WILL RETURN** AND PUNISH	HIDDEN MANNA, WHITE STONE WITH NEW NAME ON IT
THYATIRA	SON OF GOD, EYES LIKE FIRE, FEET LIKE BRONZE	GOOD WORKS, LOVE, FAITH, PERSEVERANCE, INCREASED MINISTRY	DEEPER INTO OCCULT TEACHING, IDOLATRY, AND IMMORALITY	HOLD ON TO WHAT YOU HAVE UNTIL **JESUS RETURNS**	RULE NATIONS (i.e., millennial kingdom), MORNING STAR
SARDIS	HOLDS THE 7 SPIRITS AND THE 7 STARS	NONE	MOSTLY DEAD CHURCH, DEEDS UNFINISHED	WAKE UP! STRENGTHEN WHAT REMAINS, REPENT OR **JESUS WILL RETURN LIKE A THIEF**	WHITE/PURE CLOTHES, NAME IN BOOK OF LIFE
PHILADELPHIA	HOLY AND TRUE, HOLDS KEY OF DAVID (sovereignly opens/shuts)	KEPT GOD'S WORD EVEN THOUGH HAD LITTLE STRENGTH, WIDE OPEN DOOR OF EFFECTIVE MINISTRY	NONE	HOLD FAST TO THE FAITH, **JESUS IS COMING SOON**	KEPT FROM HOUR OF TRIAL (i.e., tribulation), CROWN, MADE A PILLAR IN THE TEMPLE, NAME OF GOD, NAME OF CITY OF GOD, AND JESUS'S NEW NAME ON THEM
LAODICEA	THE AMEN, FAITHFUL/TRUE WITNESS, RULER OF CREATION	NONE	MATERIALLY WEALTHY BUT SPIRITUALLY LUKEWARM, WRETCHED, POOR, BLIND, NAKED	REPENT, GET TRUE RICHES, CLEANSING, AND SIGHT FROM JESUS **JESUS STANDS AT THE DOOR** (i.e., coming very soon)	SALVATION/FELLOWSHIP STILL POSSIBLE, SIT WITH JESUS ON THRONE

Levels of Application

There are at least four levels of application related to John's seven letters: literal, corporate, personal, and prophetic.

Literal

These letters were received by seven literal churches—historical evidence backs up the fact they existed. The commendations and corrections given by Jesus were directly applicable to these real-time churches in John's day.

Corporate

The repeated phrase "hear what the Spirit says to the churches" informs us that the instructions given to each of these ancient churches also apply to churches everywhere throughout the church age. The seven letters serve as a baseline or standard by which all other churches can evaluate their effectiveness.

Personal

The repeated phrase "whoever has ears, let them hear" clues us in that these seven letters can also serve to help every believer evaluate their own personal effectiveness. We are called to be salt and light (Matthew 5:13-16). Salt preserves, flavors, and heals. Light shines in a dark place. These seven letters help us to evaluate how salty and shiny we are as Christians.

Prophetic

As the church era marched on, students of Revelation began to notice another deeper level of application. In hindsight, they realized that the descriptions of these seven churches also lined up remarkably with seven distinct chronological periods of church history.

While not all scholars agree that this additional prophetic interpretation is valid, the more I study this personally, the more convinced I am of the importance, relevance, and accuracy of the prophetic application of these chapters. Of the 22 chapters in Revelation, chapters 2–3 have the most application for us today. Many people miss this hidden gem and gloss over these chapters to get to Revelation 4, where the dramatic end-time action begins. An in-depth study of Revelation 2–3 and how those chapters line up with church history could easily be an entire book by itself.

With that perspective in mind, consider the chart below, which details each major period of church history and its corresponding church from Revelation chapters 2–3. Keep in mind that the key features of each church period do not apply to every church or every believer during that time span. It simply means that these are the key features that characterize each period in a broad yet historically accurate sense. And there is always a remnant of true believers in each church age, no matter how negative the age may be. In Matthew 16:18, Jesus promised that his church would never disappear.

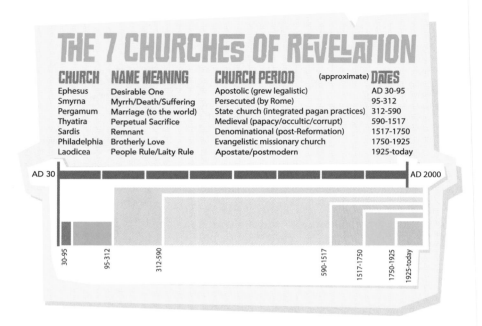

THE 7 CHURCHES OF REVELATION

CHURCH	NAME MEANING	CHURCH PERIOD	(approximate) DATES
Ephesus	Desirable One	Apostolic (grew legalistic)	AD 30-95
Smyrna	Myrrh/Death/Suffering	Persecuted (by Rome)	95-312
Pergamum	Marriage (to the world)	State church (integrated pagan practices)	312-590
Thyatira	Perpetual Sacrifice	Medieval (papacy/occultic/corrupt)	590-1517
Sardis	Remnant	Denominational (post-Reformation)	1517-1750
Philadelphia	Brotherly Love	Evangelistic missionary church	1750-1925
Laodicea	People Rule/Laity Rule	Apostate/postmodern	1925-today

AD 30 — AD 2000

30-95 95-312 312-590 590-1517 1517-1750 1750-1925 1925-today

It is interesting to note that letters to the last five churches—Pergamos, Thyatira, Sardis, Philadelphia, and Laodicea—each include statements about the Lord's return while the churches still existed. Elements from these five periods of church history also happen to still be in existence today.

The apostolic church period (represented by Ephesus) ended when the apostles died. The persecuted church period (represented by Smyrna) ended when Constantine became a Christian—or claimed to be one for pragmatic reasons—ending state-sanctioned persecution and paving the way for Christianity to be among the religions recognized by the Roman Empire. During this period, pagan practices were merged with Christian beliefs and these practices carried on into the medieval Catholic Church. This was the era of the inquisitions (prophetically connected to Jezebel from 1 and 2 Kings and specifically mentioned in Revelation 2:20).

For my Catholic friends, don't worry. I'm about to pick on my Protestant friends as well. Jesus also had some harsh words for the church of Sardis, which I believe represents the Reformation and the denominational churches that followed. While key reforms were made through Martin Luther, John Calvin, John Knox, and others, not all that came out of the Reformation era was good. Some of the denominations prompted by the Reformation grew apostate or merged with the government and were just as devoid of the Holy Spirit as was the medieval church.

Though the Reformation helped the church emerge from the Dark Ages intact, some denominations with roots in the Reformation era have since become a shell of what they once were—devoid of the vibrant life that once ignited them. Replacement theology (the belief that the church completely replaces Israel) and anti-Semitism (even from great reformers like Martin Luther) were among the errors that still needed reform after the initial escape from the dark era that preceded.

For various reasons, beginning around 1925 (and culminating fully in the late 1960s), the fired-up missionary church began to morph into more of a cultural club than a Spirit-filled organism. In mainline denominations, the authority of Scripture was undermined and Christian practice started to become more of an outward cultural aspect of life rather than an inwardly driven, thriving faith. Increased wealth and comfort in Western churches led to less of a need to rely on an unseen God. Self-sufficiency and personal rights replaced a Spirit-led walk and submission to God's will and purposes.

Remember, this does not apply to all churches or all believers. In each church era, there is always a remnant of passionately devoted believers. The Philadelphia church will still be present when the rapture occurs. I know many churches and believers who are not lukewarm, but there are also areas of Christendom today that bear a resemblance to this end-times church characterized by apathy, a trust in comfort and riches, and outward cultural motives. Many once-great denominations and seminaries are now largely devoid of biblical truth. Core Christian beliefs are frequently explained away. Sadly, even in evangelical circles we find that the reliability of Scripture, the relevance of the entire Bible, the truth of God's future judgment and the reality of hell, and many other key doctrines are currently under attack.

Overlapping Church Periods and the Return of Christ

Once the apostles died and the early persecuted church era ended, from that point forward, each church period has continued on in some discernable form to this very day. The prophetic interpretation of Revelation 2 and 3 indicates characteristics of the last five churches will still be in existence in some form when the rapture occurs, with the last church (Laodicea) being most prominent. Consider this chart showing Jesus's statements about his return.

THE 7 CHURCHES OF REVELATION

CHURCH	SECOND COMING STATEMENTS	SCRIPTURE	
Ephesus	No mention of his return/ended in 1st century		RETURN IS CLOSER WITH EACH CHURCH
Smyrna	No mention of his return/ended in 1st century		
Pergamum	Repent therefore! Otherwise, **I will soon come to you**.	Revelation 2:16	
Thyatira	Hold on to what you have **until I come**.	Revelation 2:25	
Sardis	If you do not wake up, **I will come like a thief**.	Revelation 3:3	
Philadelphia	I will keep you from the hour of trial. **I am coming soon**.	Revelation 3:10-11	
Laodicea	Here I am! **I stand at the door and knock.***	Revelation 3:20	

*Cross-reference: Matthew 24:33—Even so, when you see all these things, you know that it is near, right at the door.

What Does This Mean for Us?

We're not living in the first century, so why should we spend time dissecting these seven letters? As we analyze them and consider their various levels of interpretation, there are several practical lessons we can gain from them.

First, we need to evaluate our own lives and the culture of our churches against the commendations and corrections of the seven letters. Have we lost our passion for reaching the lost and become a bit legalistic, like the church at Ephesus? Can we learn how to live out our faith boldly even in the face of growing persecution, like the church at Smyrna? Are we carefully studying and protecting Bible doctrines so we don't drift into false teaching, like the church at Pergamum did? Are we guarding against the influence of the world so that we don't lower our standards of morality, like the church at Thyatira? Do we have a real, thriving, committed relationship to the Lord, or are we just going through the motions as cultural Christians, like the church at Sardis? Do we have an evangelistic great-commission mindset, like the church at Philadelphia? Have we become lukewarm in our faith, like the self-sufficient church at Laodicea? These are practical questions we can prayerfully wrestle with. By studying these seven letters, we can form a set of guidelines that help us evaluate how we are doing in our spiritual growth.

Second, when we understand the prophetic application of the seven letters, it becomes apparent that we are living in the last era of church history. We are living in the days of the lukewarm church of Laodicea. Generally speaking, biblical Christianity is receding from many of its strongholds. Pockets of revival still exist, as do thriving Philadelphia-like churches, but the past 40-50 years have witnessed a severe decline of biblical Christianity in the West along with the rise of secularism, the occult, atheism, New Age beliefs, and other worldly philosophies that are competing for people's attention. Europe is almost completely secular, and recent studies (such as Barna's 2017 "Competing Worldviews Influence Today's Christians" study[1]) show that the number of people in America who hold to a solidly biblical worldview is at an all-time low (only 17 percent according to the study cited above) and continues to decline.

While all this may sound depressing, we can view it as a clear sign that the most amazing event of church history is just around the corner. In the next chapter, we'll talk about this event and its implications for us today. Revelation 4 opens with a bang and shines further light on the culmination of the seven church periods. Turn the page and buckle up—things are about to get interesting!

CHAPTER 4

Snatched Away!

After this I looked, and there before me was a door standing open in heaven. And the voice I had first heard speaking to me like a trumpet said, "Come up here, and I will show you what must take place after this." At once I was in the Spirit, and there before me was a throne in heaven with someone sitting on it.

REVELATION 4:1-2

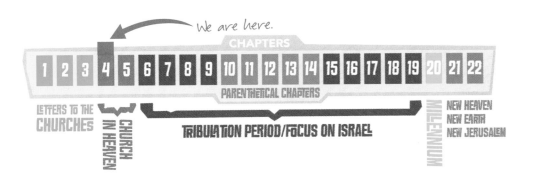

We are here.

CHAPTERS

1 2 3 4 5 6 7 8 9 10 11 12 13 14 15 16 17 18 19 20 21 22

PARENTHETICAL CHAPTERS

LETTERS TO THE CHURCHES

CHURCH IN HEAVEN

TRIBULATION PERIOD/FOCUS ON ISRAEL

MILLENNIUM

NEW HEAVEN
NEW EARTH
NEW JERUSALEM

The bride waited anxiously. Her excitement grew with each passing day because she knew her groom would show up soon—with his best man announcing their sudden arrival. She hadn't seen him since their engagement. She knew the time for his arrival was nearing, and her anticipation swelled with each passing day.

The groom's father had paid a great price—the *mohar*—for her hand in marriage. Because the bride's family was losing a vital member of the household, this custom seemed only fair. Their

engagement was a legally binding event. It wasn't a question of *if* her groom would come for her—only *when*.

Back at the father's house the son was hard at work, building the addition that he and his future bride would live in. The father observed carefully as his son lovingly crafted the new living quarters. It would initially serve as the honeymoon suite—to be enjoyed for the traditional seven days after the wedding ceremony. The father thoughtfully estimated the time needed for everything to be perfectly ready. He set a date in his mind. Only he knew the exact day he would send his son to go fetch his bride.

At the house of the bride, those who were carefully watching events unfold knew the arrival of the groom could happen at any moment. Knowing that the time for this significant event was drawing close, the bride readied herself. Bags were packed. Wedding dress was made ready. Lamp was filled with oil. The wick was lit. Hugs were given. Tears of joy and life-transition were shed. One night passed, and no groom yet. But it had to be close. Then another. Then another. Just when she thought she could wait no longer—it happened!

A trumpet and a shout to the bride from the best man broke the quiet of night from the far side of the family field. The bride rushed out to see. *Could this be it? Is this really happening?* she thought. By the time she reached the field, the few who were watching went out to join the celebration and witness the sudden snatching away of the bride. Her groom swept her into his arms and looked her in the eyes. "Never again will we be apart," he whispered. "Come, let me show you what I have made for you."

A Picture of the Rapture

Ancient Jewish wedding traditions portray a clear type or picture of the rapture.

God the Father paid the *mohar*. He gave his "only begotten" Son as the payment for our sins. The church is known in the New Testament as the bride of Christ. Jesus said he was going to prepare a place for us (see John 14:3 on the next page). He's been preparing this place for his bride for 2,000 years. Unfortunately, many who were watching have fallen asleep. The promised return of the groom eventually became a myth in their minds.

JEWISH WEDDING TRADITIONS
AND THE RAPTURE

BETROTHAL	LEAVE FATHER'S HOUSE	JESUS LEFT HEAVEN
	TRAVEL TO DESIRED BRIDE'S HOME	CAME TO EARTH AS A BABY
	PAY A GREAT PRICE FOR THE BRIDE	DIED ON THE CROSS FOR OUR SINS
	OFFER ACCEPTED OR REJECTED	OFFERS SALVATION TO US
	MARRIAGE CONTRACT/LEGALLY BOUND TOGETHER	IF WE ACCEPT WE BECOME THE CHURCH ("BRIDE OF CHRIST")
	GROOM BACK TO FATHER'S HOUSE TO PREPARE HOME	JESUS WENT BACK TO PREPARE A PLACE FOR US
WEDDING	FATHER SENDS SON BACK WHEN ALL IS READY	GOD KNOWS THE "DAY AND HOUR" HE WILL SEND THE SON
	GROOMSMEN ANNOUNCE GROOM'S ARRIVAL	THE ARCHANGEL WILL SHOUT AND A TRUMPET WILL BLOW
	BRIDE IMMEDIATELY TAKEN BACK WITH GROOM	THE CHURCH/BRIDE OF CHRIST WILL BE RAPTURED
	THE TWO ENTER WEDDING CHAMBER FOR 7 DAYS	THE CHURCH WILL BE IN HEAVEN DURING THE TRIBULATION
	GREAT WEDDING FEAST AT END OF 7 DAYS	THE CHURCH WILL ATTEND THE WEDDING FEAST OF THE LAMB

(Right side labels: 1ST COMING OF CHRIST; RAPTURE AND CHURCH IN HEAVEN DURING TRIBULATION PERIOD)

As for those who are still awake, just when we think we can no longer wait—perhaps very soon—the Father will send the Son to fetch his bride. Jesus told us in advance that this would be the condition of the church when he returned. In Matthew 24:44 he said, "You also must be ready, because the Son of Man will come at an hour when you do not expect him." The sad fact is that many Christians will not be expecting the rapture even though we are given many signs to indicate its proximity (Matthew 24–25; Mark 13; Luke 21).

Revelation chapter 4 opens with this future event. After two full chapters of Jesus directly addressing the church (with 19 uses of the word *church*), we discover an abrupt shift as John describes an open door, a call from heaven, and a sudden change of location. Within an instant, John found himself in the very throne room of God. From that point on, the word *church* is absent from the rest of the book of Revelation. This supports the notion that the church will be caught up to heaven prior to the seven-year tribulation period. Let's take a quick look at the primary rapture texts in Scripture so we can have the details fresh in our minds as we read about this breathtaking opening of Revelation 4.

The Primary Rapture Texts

1 Corinthians 15:51-53

> Listen, I tell you a mystery: We will not all sleep, but we will all be changed—in a flash, in the twinkling of an eye, at the last trumpet. For the trumpet will sound, the dead will be raised imperishable, and we will be changed. For the perishable must clothe itself with the imperishable, and the mortal with immortality.

1 Thessalonians 4:16-18

> The Lord himself will come down from heaven, with a loud command, with the voice of the archangel and with the trumpet call of God, and the dead in Christ will rise first. After that, we who are still alive and are left will be caught up together with them in the clouds to meet the Lord in the air. And so we will be with the Lord forever. Therefore encourage one another with these words.

Revelation 3:10

> Since you have kept my command to endure patiently, I will also keep you from the hour of trial that is going to come on the whole world to test the inhabitants of the earth.

John 14:3

> If I go and prepare a place for you, I will come back and take you to be with me that you also may be where I am.

When we study these primary rapture texts we discover several important facts that help shed light on what is taking place at the beginning of Revelation 4. At the rapture, all church-age believers (alive and dead) will be given bodies fit for heaven as we meet the Lord in the air. We learn from Revelation 3:10 and other passages of Scripture that this great escape will occur before the tribulation period. This fact should bring great encouragement to believers (1 Thessalonians 4:18). We find the chronology of the early chapters of Revelation lining up perfectly with what we know about the rapture. If Revelation 2 and 3 depict the church age, then it is fitting for the rapture of the church to be depicted immediately following the final church era. Revelation 4 opens with this momentous event.

The New Location of the Lampstands

Another interesting fact that supports the idea that Revelation 4 depicts the rapture is that the lampstands we read about in chapters 2–3, which clearly depict the churches, are now seen in heaven as a Holy Spirit–inhabited menorah that blazes before God's throne.[1] Revelation 1:20 specifically informs us that "the seven lampstands are the seven churches." We also know from Scripture that the Holy Spirit indwells each true believer—each member of the worldwide church.

After the open door and the trumpet call to "come up here" we find that the lampstands and the Holy Spirit are seen in the throne room of God. In Revelation 4:5 we read, "In front of the throne, seven lamps were blazing. These are the seven spirits of God."

QUICK FACT: DID YOU KNOW...

that the number 7 represents fullness or completion?
The Holy Spirit's key role as a comforter during the church age will be all done when the church is raptured and enters heaven.

Isaiah 11:2-3 describes seven aspects of the Holy Spirit's ministry. There we read, "The *Spirit of the LORD* will rest on him—the *Spirit of wisdom* and of *understanding*, the *Spirit of counsel* and of *might*, the *Spirit of the knowledge* and *fear of the*

Lord—and he will delight in the fear of the Lord" (emphasis added). As we compare Scripture with Scripture, we can make sense of the symbols in Revelation and stand in awe at the unity and design of the Bible as a whole.

We learn from 2 Thessalonians 2:7, in Paul's description of the Antichrist, that the restraining power of the Holy Spirit—which is present on earth through the church—is what currently prevents the lawless spirit of Antichrist from taking over. But the moment that the church—and the indwelling Holy Spirit with her—is removed and taken to heaven, the stage will be set for all hell to break loose on the earth. We see this joint symbolism of the church and the Holy Spirit clearly depicted in Revelation 4 as the lampstands are physically moved from earth to heaven—a depiction of the rapture.

The Jewishness of Revelation

In addition to the curious absence of the church after the opening verse of chapter 4, we also find that the focus of God's redemptive attention shifts back to Israel, the Jewish people, and the city of Jerusalem. As I mentioned earlier, within the 404 verses of Revelation there are more than 800 direct references or allusions to the Old Testament.[2] Keeping this in mind as you study Revelation will help bring even more clarity to its pages.

CHAPTERS

6 7 8 9 10 11 12 13 14 15 16 17 18 19

TRIBULATION PERIOD/FOCUS ON ISRAEL

There are at least four main purposes of God's judgment during the tribulation period:

1. Punishment of the world's sin after a long period of grace.

2. To spur Israel and the Jewish people to turn to Christ for salvation and see that he is indeed their long-awaited Messiah.

3. To cause a remnant of tribulation-period Gentiles to come to the Lord.

4. To usher in the return of Christ to earth to set up the millennial kingdom.

It is the second reason above that I would like to call to your attention. It is directly related to the details of a yet-unfulfilled prophecy in Daniel chapter 9. To understand Revelation, it's critically important to understand Daniel 9, which describes seventy sets of seven years, the last of which constitutes the seven-year tribulation period detailed in Revelation. A basic understanding of the last four verses of Daniel 9 provides the full scope of Jewish history from Daniel's day until the end. It is also the clear framework into which all other tribulation details fit.

Daniel 9:24-27 speaks of "sevens" for sets of seven years. The use of the term "sevens" is similar to how we would speak of "decades" for sets of ten years. We see the precedent for a week being viewed as seven years in Genesis 29:28, where Jacob worked seven years to marry Rachel and this time span is referred to as her "week." Here is what we read in these four critical verses in Daniel 9:

> Seventy "sevens" are decreed for your people and your holy city to finish transgression, to put an end to sin, to atone for wickedness, to bring in everlasting righteousness, to seal up vision and prophecy and to anoint the Most Holy Place. Know and understand this: From the time the word goes out to restore and rebuild Jerusalem until the Anointed One, the ruler, comes, there will be seven "sevens," and sixty-two "sevens." It will be rebuilt with streets and a

trench, but in times of trouble. After the sixty-two "sevens," the Anointed One will be put to death and will have nothing. The people of the ruler who will come will destroy the city and the sanctuary. The end will come like a flood: War will continue until the end, and desolations have been decreed. He will confirm a covenant with many for one "seven." In the middle of the "seven" he will put an end to sacrifice and offering. And at the temple he will set up an abomination that causes desolation, until the end that is decreed is poured out on him.

This section of Daniel chapter 9 (the 70 "weeks" of years) points to 69 "weeks" of years that begin with the command to rebuild Jerusalem (the command by Artaxerxes in 457 BC—Ezra 7:12-26) and end with "Messiah the Prince" entering Jerusalem (Palm Sunday) 490 years later (Daniel 9:25 NKJV). According to experts who have taken the time to do the math, this prophecy was literally fulfilled not just to the year, but to the exact day.

Daniel 9:26 tells us that the Messiah will be "cut off, but not for Himself" (NKJV). This was strange and cryptic language until Jesus died on the cross. Now we understand this was a reference to Jesus's sacrificial death on the cross to save us from our sins.

After 69 "weeks" (of years), we notice an indefinite period of time passing by before the final "week" of 7 years. Verse 26 tells us that the temple will be destroyed (this was literally fulfilled in AD 70 when Roman soldiers tore down the temple). But then in verse 27 we read that a future ruler will "put an end to sacrifice and offering" and set up an abomination in the temple. This necessitates the rebuilding of the temple during the end times (currently in full planning mode by The Temple Institute, which is located in Jerusalem). Revelation and the Olivet Discourse in Matthew 24–25 provide more details, indicating this new temple must be rebuilt by the middle of the tribulation period. We now understand (from this and other passages) that the indefinite period of time, or the church age, fits into the gap between the two temple events.

The 70 weeks of Daniel 9 tell how God is working out his plan for the Jewish people during the first 69 sets of 7 years. When Jesus came at his first advent, the Jewish prophetic clock paused for the church age. At some future date, the church will be taken out of the picture via the rapture. Soon after, the tribulation period will begin. It will be initiated by the signing or enforcing of a treaty between Israel and the antichrist. This event will cause the Jewish prophetic clock to start again so it can complete the last set of 7 years—which is also the duration of the tribulation period. During this time, God's attention will turn back to the Jews and Israel. Later we will learn more about 2 Jewish witnesses, 144,000 Jewish evangelists, and the entire world being hyper-focused on Jerusalem. At the midpoint of the tribulation, the antichrist will turn against the Jewish people and persecute them as never before. If you keep all of this in mind as you study Revelation, it will make much more sense.

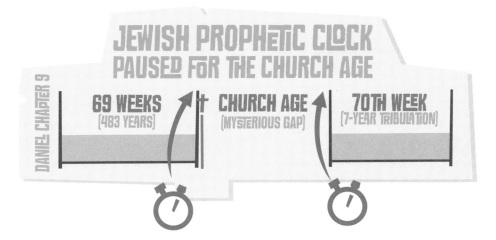

Next Stop—The Throne Room

After the incredible opening verse of Revelation 4, the rest of the chapter describes the jaw-dropping scene in the throne room of heaven. In this detailed account we see a heavenly throne with a figure sitting on it, circled by a reflective glowing rainbow, sitting before a blazing Holy Spirit-filled menorah, surrounded by four indescribable creatures and twenty-four elders on thrones. At the feet of the one on the throne is what John describes as a "sea of glass" and later says also has the characteristics of fire (Revelation 15:2). In Revelation 8:3 we learn there is an altar in the throne room, which lets us know this room is also a heavenly temple.

QUICK FACT: DID YOU KNOW...

that the 24 elders* in the throne room most likely represent the church? These figures are not depicted in the Old Testament visions of God's throne room found in Isaiah, Ezekiel, or Daniel. They show up only here in Revelation after the rapture of the church (Revelation 4) and they are depicted on thrones, wearing white robes and crowns—all specific rewards cited by Jesus in the letters to the 7 churches.

*They may also be the 12 patriarchs and the 12 apostles.

Psalm 11:4—The Lord is in his holy temple; the Lord is on his heavenly throne. He observes everyone on earth; his eyes examine them.

The four indescribable angelic creatures give praise to the one on the throne as the twenty-four elders lay down their crowns in total worship. As the creatures and the elders give praise, lightning and thunder burst forth from the throne. It is a scene of incredible awe and majesty. No level of computer graphics imagery, surround sound, virtual reality, or immersion technology could come close to capturing what John saw after he was caught up to heaven. John used the word "like" repeatedly in this account. He did his best to put this scene into words, but words couldn't do any justice—what John saw was impossible to describe.

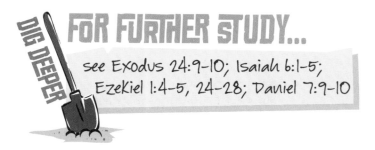

DIG DEEPER FOR FURTHER STUDY...

see Exodus 24:9-10; Isaiah 6:1-5; Ezekiel 1:4-5, 24-28; Daniel 7:9-10

Truly Awesome

The word *awesome* is so overused that it has lost its punch in American culture since its 1980s pop-culture proliferation. The root meaning is "awe-inspiring."

Most of the time we use *awesome* to mean that something is exceptionally good—like a meal, a song, or a vacation. The original meaning of the word has more weight. Some synonyms are *breathtaking, staggering, indescribable*—like trying to describe the Grand Canyon, Mount Everest, or the power of an atomic bomb. Our future rapture-induced trip to heaven's throne room will be truly awesome.

According to 1 Corinthians 15:53, when we are raptured, we will be changed in an instant—"the perishable must clothe itself with the imperishable." The reason this must happen is that we cannot handle the awesome realities of heaven in our current bodies. At the moment of the rapture, we will receive glorified heavenly bodies that *can* handle the sights, sounds, emotions, and knowledge of heaven.

Revelation chapter 4 highlights the sudden and unparalleled change we will experience at the rapture, when we suddenly find ourselves called up and transformed so we can enter the very throne room of heaven. There, we will join in the worship of the one who sits on the heavenly throne—the King of all kings. I can't wait—it is going to be truly awesome!

CHAPTER 5

The Tribulation Begins

I saw in the right hand of him who sat on the throne a scroll with writing on both sides and sealed with seven seals. And I saw a mighty angel proclaiming in a loud voice, "Who is worthy to break the seals and open the scroll?" But no one in heaven or on earth or under the earth could open the scroll or even look inside it. I wept and wept because no one was found who was worthy to open the scroll or look inside. Then one of the elders said to me, "Do not weep! See, the Lion of the tribe of Judah, the Root of David, has triumphed. He is able to open the scroll and its seven seals."

REVELATION 5:1-5

We have already established the basic past-present-future outline of Revelation. You and I currently live during the last phase of church history as we await the imminent (any moment) rapture of the church, which will serve as the catalyst for all that follows. At the conclusion of our study of Revelation 4, we found John and the church in the very throne room of God.

Enemy Territory

There's one key fact about the rapture that I didn't mention in the previous chapter. This amazing future event will be a special-ops invasion into Satan's territory. The enemy's success in luring Adam and Eve into sin had massive implications far beyond a couple of bites missing from a piece of forbidden fruit.

Mankind was given dominion over the earth, then lost it to Satan when Adam and Eve sinned. Creation itself was cursed and has been "groaning as in the pains of childbirth" (Romans 8:22) ever since as it awaits a future day of redemption. The grand sweep of biblical history can be seen as a three-part process: creation, fall, redemption. After creation, man sinned, and the earth fell under the rule of Satan. He's known as the "prince of the power of the air" and the "god of this age," among other things (Ephesians 2:2 NKJV; 2 Corinthians 4:4). In the New Testament we find Satan tempting Jesus with "all the kingdoms of the world" (Luke 4:5). Scriptural evidence supports the idea that Satan's proposal was a legitimate offer.

The Enemy's Three-Part Fall

Satan's leash is given its length by a sovereign God who allows evil to exist for a time and for a purpose. It is confusing for us when we try to understand why God allows evil to exist, but we know the reasons will make full sense when all is said and done. This temporary allowance of evil is directly linked to the necessity of free will—and free will is necessary to demonstrate love. Free will is essential so that people can choose whom they will serve. Love can be demonstrated only by permitting free will. Forced love is no love at all. The risk of free will is that people can choose to rebel. Such was the case with Satan and the one-third of the angels who rebelled with him in a past age.

Satan was given the highest level of angelic rank. When he and one-third of the multitude of angels rebelled, they were kicked out of heaven. In the book of Job and a few other places in Scripture, we find that Satan still has access to heaven's council, though he is no longer a citizen. In the middle of the tribulation period (which we'll study in a later chapter), Satan will be cast down to Earth. At the end of the tribulation he will be bound for 1,000 years, during the millennial kingdom. After that, he will be released for one last rebellion. Following this epic rematch where Satan is once again handily defeated, the ancient evil figure will be thrown into the Lake of Fire—a permanent destination of punishment created specifically for Satan and the fallen angels.

Creation's Three-Part Redemption

There is also a three-part process to God's plan for redemption. First, our spiritual redemption was secured at the cross. Next, our future physical redemption will occur at the moment of the rapture. And finally, the earth will be redeemed and restored to its original state when God creates a new heaven and a new earth after the future millennial kingdom. But first, the earth must be reclaimed.

In Revelation 5, we find John weeping because when a search was made, it seemed that no one was found worthy to redeem the earth. Just when all hope seems lost, one of the 24 elders from the church age will remind the heavenly council of the ancient prophetic names of the Messiah—the Lion of the tribe of Judah, and the Root of David. The elder will point out the fact that the Messiah has already triumphed. Then Jesus will appear as the Lamb who took away the sins of the world, and because he is the victor, he will possess the rightful authority to reclaim the earth.

Why the initial pouring out of tears? If no one was found worthy enough to open the scroll, the earth would remain under the curse and Satan's dominion, God's plans for the redemption of Israel would not be secured, and he would be found to have broken his word regarding specific future prophecies and promises. In short, evil would win.

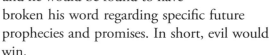

Earlier I highlighted the important link between the symbolism in Revelation and the Old Testament. Here in Revelation 5, we find the Trinity at work (Father on the throne, Son taking the scroll from the Father, Holy Spirit present in his sevenfold fullness) all in the same scene. The scroll depicted here is the title deed to the earth. The Father is the judge. Satan is the current ruler of the earth. Jesus is shown to be the qualified kinsman-redeemer.

The Kinsman-Redeemer Reclaims the Earth

In the Old Testament (Leviticus 25 and the book of Ruth, for example), God established a system whereby a relative could marry a woman who was widowed, free a relative who became a debt-slave, and buy back land that was lost due to debt. This "kinsman-redeemer," as the Bible calls him, had to be a close relative from the same tribe, possess the means to pay off the debt that was owed, and be willing to pay off the debt and be the kinsman-redeemer. All three elements of being a kinsman-redeemer were ultimately tied to land ownership.

When someone had to turn over his land to pay off a debt, the terms were written on a scroll by a judge, and the scroll was rolled up and sealed with hot wax. At this point, the property was officially transferred to the creditor. The contract would remain sealed and in the judge's possession until the debt could be paid by the debtor or a kinsman-redeemer.

When mankind fell into sin, the earth was temporarily deeded to Satan. Jesus, the Kinsman-Redeemer, paid our debt, and we are no longer slaves to sin. He fulfilled the expensive requirements of the *mohar* (or dowry) for the church at  his death and resurrection and will one day complete this redemptive act when he whisks his bride away at the rapture.

Immediately after that all-important event, Jesus—the Kinsman-Redeemer—will take the title deed from the judge's hand and officially reclaim the rights to the earth. The only problem is, Satan is a greedy landowner who does not give up territory willingly. The law means nothing to him, so Jesus will have to take his land by force. This is one of the primary reasons for, and purposes of, the tribulation period.

Praise God that we have a Kinsman-Redeemer who is worthy, willing, and able to redeem the bride and the land! The rest of Revelation 5 depicts an ever-expanding and contagious succession of praise celebrating this fact. Once again, when all seems lost, God will come through for humanity, and the resulting worship in the throne room of God will ignite a ripple effect of praise unlike any the universe has ever seen.

The Seals of the Title Deed Are Opened

Chapter 6 of Revelation begins the section that most people are familiar with. The tribulation period opens with the famous four horsemen of the apocalypse. The tribulation is described in Revelation chapters 6–19. We are given a chronological description of events with some parenthetical chapters and sections that provide

more information and backstory as to what is taking place during the tribulation. For the most part Revelation is written chronologically, but it includes passages that allow the reader to pause and gain further details about certain themes. In this way, Revelation is somewhat like a novel or a well-crafted movie.

Seal Judgment 1: The White Horse

Revelation 6:1-2—I watched as the Lamb opened the first of the seven seals. Then I heard one of the four living creatures say in a voice like thunder, "Come!" I looked, and there before me was a white horse! Its rider held a bow, and he was given a crown, and he rode out as a conqueror bent on conquest.

At the moment of the rapture (Revelation 4:1), chaos will immediately engulf the world as suddenly unmanned planes, trains, and automobiles crash and millions go missing. With the restraining influence of the Holy Spirit and the church now out of the picture, evil will capitalize on this long-awaited set of circumstances. The ensuing global disorder will lead the nations to cry out for a man-with-a-plan.

QUICK FACT: DID YOU KNOW...

that Paul-Henri Spaak (1899–1972), former Belgian prime minister and one of the original architects of what has since morphed into the European Union, is credited with saying, "We do not want another committee, we have too many already. What we want is a man of sufficient stature to hold the allegiance of all people, and to lift us out of the economic morass into which we are sinking. Send us such a man, and be he god or devil, we will receive him"?

Source: David Jeremiah, *What in the World Is Going On?: 10 Prophetic Clues You Cannot Afford to Ignore* (Nashville, TN: Thomas Nelson, 2008), 65.

This may also be the opportune moment for Russia, Iran, and Turkey to lead the prophesied Ezekiel 38 war against Israel. We're not told the exact timing of this future war other than the fact it will be during the last days, when Israel dwells securely. The instability and power vacuum caused by the rapture will surely lead various evil world leaders to pounce on this once-in-a-lifetime opportunity to expand their powers.

EZEKIEL 38 NATIONS
AND THEIR MODERN-DAY EQUIVALENTS

ANCIENT NAME	MODERN NAME
MAGOG	RUSSIA, CENTRAL ASIA
ROSH	RUSSIA
MESHECH	RUSSIA
TUBAL	RUSSIA OR TURKEY
PERSIA	IRAN
CUSH	ETHIOPIA, SUDAN
LUD	LIBYA, ALGERIA
GOMER	TURKEY
TOGARMAH	TURKEY, CENTRAL ASIA

Many experts agree that this end-time battle will likely occur just before the tribulation begins or as part of the second seal judgment when war breaks out on earth. The main reasons for this assessment include:

1. After the war, Israel will use the weapons of the enemy (possibly nuclear) for energy for seven years (Ezekiel 39:9).

2. In Ezekiel 38:18, we find that this battle seems to be the tipping point for God's wrath. The verse informs us that "in that day" (that is, the day of the Lord, or the tribulation period), Gog's attack will arouse God's "hot anger" and "fiery wrath" (verses 18-19).

3. God will once again display great miracles as he supernaturally destroys Israel's enemies, making himself "known in the sight of many nations" (verse 23).

It's important to note that the elements needed for this future war are currently in place due to a convergence of recent events stemming from the Syrian civil war, which began in 2011. For the first time in history, all the prophesied nations are aligned on both sides of the equation, and the key players (Russia, Iran, Turkey) are in an official partnership with troops and interests in Syria, just north of Israel—exactly where this end-time attack is prophesied to originate from.

We understand from Daniel chapters 2 and 7, as well as Revelation chapters 13 and 17, that the rider on the white horse is none other than the antichrist. The term *anti* means "against," and it can also mean "in place of." This evil end-time ruler will be a false messiah and will appear on the scene after the rapture.

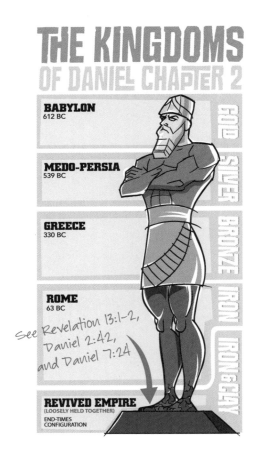

THE KINGDOMS
OF DANIEL CHAPTER 2

BABYLON
612 BC

MEDO-PERSIA
539 BC

GREECE
330 BC

ROME
63 BC

See Revelation 13:1-2,
Daniel 2:42,
and Daniel 7:24

REVIVED EMPIRE
(LOOSELY HELD TOGETHER)
END-TIMES
CONFIGURATION

GOLD SILVER BRONZE IRON IRON & CLAY

The event that will officially begin the seven-year tribulation and identify the antichrist will be the confirming of a treaty put into place by this new, seemingly peaceful ruler. He will arise out of a ten-nation confederacy from a region that was formerly part of the ancient Roman Empire (see Revelation 13:1-2; Daniel 2:42; 7:24).

You'll notice that this future ruler will have great power and will initially seem like a remarkable peacemaker. He is depicted as having a bow without arrows, and Revelation 6:2 explains that "he was given a crown." He will be so charismatic and persuasive that global power will fall into his lap. Whether by an elective process or the decisions of a few elite figures, the antichrist's authority will be willingly and easily given to him.

Seal Judgment 2: The Red Horse

Revelation 6:3-4—When the Lamb opened the second seal, I heard the second living creature say, "Come!" Then another horse came out, a fiery red one. Its rider was given power to take peace from the earth and to make people kill each other. To him was given a large sword.

At the breaking of the second seal, peace will be taken from the earth. This could mean that the plethora of regional conflicts and threats of war that are bubbling beneath the surface in our day will finally erupt into a larger global war. However, based on the antichrist's global control achieved by the second half of the tribulation, it is more likely that the antichrist himself will take peace from the earth as he begins to conquer the unwilling by military force. This will also include the severe persecution of any newly saved tribulation-era believers, as we'll see later in this chapter.

Notice the rider of the red horse will be given a large sword. Throughout Scripture, swords symbolize military power and strength. This evil figure will have access to the strongest military weaponry ever available. This large sword could refer to nuclear capability, or perhaps something even more potent. Emerging technologies such as weaponized artificial intelligence, laser-based weapons systems, and various supersoldier programs could all factor into the equation and be a part of this great sword wielded by this evil end-time ruler.

It is important to note that while the antichrist begins his conquest and the world erupts into war, Israel will not be involved because of the peace treaty. Daniel 9:27 informs us that the antichrist will not turn on Israel until the middle of the seven-year tribulation period. We'll cover this at length in a later chapter.

Seal Judgment 3: The Black Horse

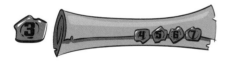

Revelation 6:5-6—When the Lamb opened the third seal, I heard the third living creature say, "Come!" I looked, and there before me was a black horse! Its rider was holding a pair of scales in his hand. Then I heard what sounded like a voice among the four living creatures, saying, "Two pounds of wheat for a day's wages, and six pounds of barley for a day's wages, and do not damage the oil and the wine!"

The logical outcome of world war is famine. As food distribution systems break down, riots shut down cities, electronic systems fail, and crops and factories are destroyed by war, famine will grip the world. Within a fairly short time, food will become scarce and prices will soar beyond anything we have experienced. Only the elite will have the means to weather this seal judgment. Oil and wine are not staples for survival; they are luxury items. As with any dictatorship, the ruling elite will enjoy abundance while vast populations starve with little to no means of finding their way out of the terrible famine conditions.

Seal Judgment 4: The Pale Horse

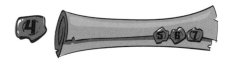

Revelation 6:7-8—When the Lamb opened the fourth seal, I heard the voice of the fourth living creature say, "Come!" I looked, and there before me was a pale horse! Its rider was named Death, and Hades was following close behind him. They were given power over a fourth of the earth to kill by sword, famine and plague, and by the wild beasts of the earth.

The breaking of the fourth seal introduces the pale horse of death. The conditions resulting from the first three seals will lead to deaths on a massive scale as war, famine, plague, and animal attacks cause one-quarter of the world's population to die. The current world population is 7.8 billion. We don't know how many people will be raptured, but one-fourth of the world's remaining population will die over the course of the first four seal judgments.

As you read Revelation, keep in mind that each judgment is added to the previous judgments, or in some cases, added to the conditions left by the previous judgments. The entire tribulation period will feature a steady increase in the severity of what takes place.

Seal Judgment 5: Martyrdom

Revelation 6:9-11—When he opened the fifth seal, I saw under the altar the souls of those who had been slain because of the word of God and the testimony they had maintained. They called out in a loud voice, "How long, Sovereign Lord, holy and true, until you judge the inhabitants of the earth and avenge our blood?" Then each of them was given a white robe, and they were told to wait a little longer, until the full number of their fellow servants, their brothers and sisters, were killed just as they had been.

In 2 Thessalonians chapter 2, Paul provides insight that the antichrist cannot be revealed until the Holy Spirit steps out of the way. There is currently a tide of evil waiting to break loose on the earth the moment the church is removed via the rapture. Unique to the church age is the fact that the Holy Spirit indwells each believer starting at the moment of salvation, and this helps to have a restraining influence on evil in the world. But once the church and the influence of the Holy Spirit are gone, evil will become unleashed and engulf the earth like a tidal wave.

There are more Christians persecuted and martyred in our day than in any other era in history. Even in the West, where Christianity has long flourished, it now wanes. Governments once founded on Judeo-Christian principles of law and order are steadily becoming antithetical or openly hostile toward their Christian roots. After Christians are raptured from the earth, the majority of the left-behind citizens of the world will celebrate their departure. Many will see the disappearances as some sort of a New Age or alien judgment designed to eradicate the close-minded, backward, and old-fashioned God-followers who were holding humanity back from "progress."

In the wake of the rapture the cultural gloves will come off, and anyone found to have become a believer in Christ will be severely persecuted or even martyred in quick fashion. Many people will become saved as they look for answers that explain the mass disappearances—they will find Bibles and Bible studies left behind, and recall the teachings of their Christian friends and family who tried to warn them. In addition, there will be 144,000 Jewish evangelists and 2 Jewish preachers in Jerusalem who will get the whole world's attention during the first half of the tribulation. Their proclamation of the gospel will draw many to receive Christ as Savior.

144K SEALED EVANGELISTS   2 WITNESSES

A great number of people will become believers during the first half of the tribulation, and according to the details about the fifth seal judgment, many will be martyred. Some Bible expositors say that the beasts mentioned in relation to the breaking of the fourth seal are evil world rulers bent on killing anyone who tries to revive the beliefs of those who had disappeared via the rapture. The antichrist and the false prophet are both described as beasts later in Revelation, so this view does have some merit. In any case, it's clear that a large number of new believers will be martyred during the earlier seal judgments. Details about the end-time empire described in Daniel 7 support this notion as well.

Seal Judgment 6: Global Megaquake

Revelation 6:12-17—I watched as he opened the sixth seal. There was a great earthquake. The sun turned black like sackcloth made of goat hair, the whole moon turned blood red, and the stars in the sky fell to earth, as figs drop from a fig tree when shaken by a strong wind. The heavens receded like a scroll being rolled up, and every mountain and island was removed from its place. Then the kings of the earth, the princes, the generals, the rich, the mighty, and everyone else, both slave and free, hid in caves and among the rocks of the mountains. They called to the mountains and the rocks, "Fall on us and hide us from the face of him who sits on the throne and from the wrath of the Lamb! For the great day of their wrath has come, and who can withstand it?"

The sixth seal judgment will rock the world to its core. Volcanologists and seismologists inform us that one megaquake can trigger others,[1] and geologists tell us that the earth's crust sits on a plastic-like mantle, in turn, sits on a liquid outer core.[2]

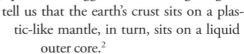

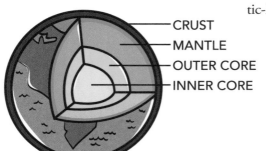

CRUST
MANTLE
OUTER CORE
INNER CORE

It appears that during the sixth seal judgment, all of the earth's fault lines will fracture in such a way as to cause a catastrophic global earthquake, which in turn will trigger volcanos to erupt. The worldwide eruptions will blacken the sky. At the same time, a massive meteor or asteroid event will occur.

In recent decades, there has been a steady increase in the frequency and intensity of seismic activity worldwide (covered in more detail in my book *The Non-Prophet's Guide™ to the End Times*), just as predicted by Jesus in the Olivet Discourse. These seismic birth pains will crescendo during the tribulation period.

Experts point out that the description of the seismic activity and the sky moving (being rolled up like a scroll) could very well indicate a partial or full crustal shift of the earth's surface. The fact that every mountain and island will be "removed" from its place seems to indicate a very significant shift of the tectonic plates upon the earth, which glide over the plastic-like mantle and the liquid outer core underneath the plates.

What would trigger such a shift? One possibility is that a large celestial object (such as a comet or asteroid) could come close enough to the earth to affect its orbit, thus causing a crustal shift. This would explain the global meteor shower that coincides with this seal judgment. In response, the world's elite and "everyone else" will look for places to hide from the terrible atmospheric and seismic conditions. We also learn from Jesus in Luke 21:26 that "people will faint from terror, apprehensive of what is coming on the world, for the heavenly bodies will be shaken."

What's interesting about people trying to hide among the rocks of the mountains is the fact that underground bunkers are in demand today. There has been an enormous spike in private, military, and secret bunker construction projects in recent years. CNN even featured an online article entitled, "Billionaire buyers: How the 1% are preparing for the apocalypse."[3]

In any case, this judgment will be so severe that it will get the attention of many of the lost. They will be in abject terror, realizing that this judgment comes directly from

God. In fear they will hide "from the face of him who sits on the throne and from the wrath of the Lamb!" (Revelation 6:16). They will acknowledge that this is indeed God's wrath being unleashed on earth.

What About the Seventh Seal?

The seventh seal is yet to come (in Revelation 8), but first, John interrupts the scene of judgment with some parenthetical information in Revelation 7. Here, he pauses to let readers catch their breath and he fills in some gaps before resuming with the seventh and final seal judgment, which will take the tribulation judgments to a whole new level.

There are several practical lessons we can learn from the future seal judgments. For starters, God is patient beyond compare, but eventually there will come a point at which evil must be punished. We're reminded that Jesus Christ is the sinless Son of God and the only one in all of history who is worthy to judge the world and make all things right. We see that God's mercy will continue after the rapture and that many will turn to God for salvation, but this news is bittersweet because this will happen during a terrible time on the earth, and most of these tribulation-era believers will be martyred for their faith. The knowledge of what is to come should move us to action now, compelling us to reach as many people as we can with the gospel of Christ.

Brand of Brothers

See, the day of the LORD is coming—a cruel day, with wrath and fierce anger—to make the land desolate and destroy the sinners within it. The stars of heaven and their constellations will not show their light. The rising sun will be darkened and the moon will not give its light. I will punish the world for its evil, the wicked for their sins. I will put an end to the arrogance of the haughty and will humble the pride of the ruthless. I will make people scarcer than pure gold, more rare than the gold of Ophir. Therefore I will make the heavens tremble; and the earth will shake from its place at the wrath of the LORD Almighty, in the day of his burning anger.

ISAIAH 13:9-13

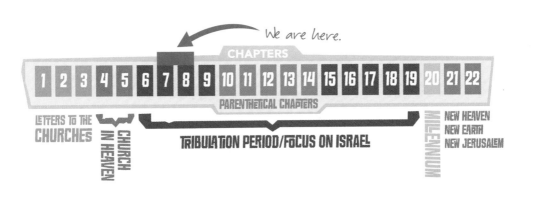

We are here.

CHAPTERS

1 2 3 4 5 6 7 8 9 10 11 12 13 14 15 16 17 18 19 20 21 22

PARENTHETICAL CHAPTERS

LETTERS TO THE CHURCHES — CHURCH IN HEAVEN — TRIBULATION PERIOD/FOCUS ON ISRAEL — MILLENNIUM — NEW HEAVEN NEW EARTH NEW JERUSALEM

I truly believe that God has his people strategically placed to accomplish his plans. I've seen this on the mission field and in other areas of ministry. It is amazing to me how many times on missions trips I've seen God's plan unfold for the team as circumstances and ministry opportunities arise that seem custom-fit for the people who are on the trip. On more than one occasion I've seen volunteers question how God was going to use them on a trip, then find themselves in a situation that was an ideal match for their specific talents, interests, and spiritual gifts.

God sovereignly positions people for strategic purposes. His purposes will stand, and in each era, those who want to join him in his work get the privilege of being placed into his unfolding plan.

In Revelation 7, we are introduced to some new characters in our story. John peels back the curtain again and introduces us to a compass of 4 angels. You might call them the angels of the north, south, east, and west. Their job is to hold back land and sea destruction until a fifth angel will "seal" a specific group of tribulation-era believers known as the 144,000 Jewish evangelists—strategically placed in time and place to accomplish a critical part of God's plan to reach people during the horrible tribulation. Even in his wrath, God will extend offers of grace and forgiveness!

We are told that this group of 144,000 is made up of 12,000 individuals from each of the 12 tribes of Israel. They will be given a seal that will protect them. They are the property of the King—marked with his brand and supernaturally protected to share the message of salvation in Christ to those left behind after the Rapture.

QUICK FACT: DID YOU KNOW...

that DNA testing can tell if a Jewish person is from the priestly tribe of the Levites?[1]

What's in a Logo?

In this case, being sealed doesn't mean being closed up in an envelope—it means "branded" or "marked." Essentially, these evangelists will have God's logo on their forehead. The logo of an organization is also known as the brand mark—a term taken from the practice of branding animals to show ownership. The brand mark is not the brand itself, but a visual representation of the brand. It is symbolic of the entire brand experience including the brand's promises, core values, mission, vision, history, and more. In short, the logo or brand mark represents the entirety of the brand. These branded tribulation-era missionaries will be special because of the God behind the seal.

If you have ever seen any of the Toy Story movies by Pixar, there's a theme that runs through them related to branding. Whenever one of the main toys needs a reminder of who they belong to, they look at the bottom of their foot, where their childhood owner, Andy, has written his name. In a similar sense, these 144,000 Jewish evangelists will be branded as the Lord's own. They will be tasked with telling the world about God's mercy and grace—still available in the midst of his wrath. What a merciful God!

The ministry of the 144,000 will lead to the salvation of multitudes of people all over the world. Beginning in Revelation 7:9, we read of a "great multitude that no one could count" who will have come out of the tribulation. The tough part is that all of them will be martyrs. Sadly, most who find salvation during the tribulation period will die for their faith. We do, however, find that these martyred tribulation saints will have a special position serving the Lord before his throne—never to suffer again.

QUICK FACT: DID YOU KNOW...

that several cults take this passage out of context and claim that their members comprise the 144,000?

Recalling the importance of Daniel chapter 9 and the prophecy of the 70 weeks of years—you'll remember that 69 of those "weeks" were fulfilled prior to the church age. Week 70, or the final week, is the tribulation period. That's when the focus shifts away from God's plan for the Gentiles in the church age and back onto the Jewish people. All of Scripture—and the Savior himself—came through the Jewish people. During the tribulation, the world will once again see God's covenant people play a key role in the world's final events. God's 4,000-year-old promise to Abraham that the whole world would be blessed through him will continue to be fulfilled during the tribulation period and beyond.

The Seventh Seal

After the account of the sealing of the 144,000 in Revelation 7, John describes the breaking of the seventh and final seal in chapter 8. The final seal judgment will initiate a dramatic pause that will set up the next set of global calamities, known as the trumpet judgments. It's important to note that the seventh judgment in each of the sets of 7 judgments (seals, trumpets, bowls) each unlock the next phase of judgment and include a proclamation (or strange silence in the case of the seventh seal), thunder, lightning, something falling from the sky, and increasingly destructive earthquake-related events.

When the seventh seal is opened, John tells us there will be silence in heaven for "about a half an hour." You'll recall from our earlier reading that heaven is filled with magnificent sounds of celebration from multitudes of angels and believers who will be singing and praising God. It will be anything but quiet there. The silence caused by the breaking of the seventh seal will be obvious—and deafening. Experts speculate about reason for the 30 minutes of silence. I honestly don't know, but I believe we will understand it at the time. One possibility is that the silence will indicate the world has reached a point of no return, and that something of major significance is about to occur.

The silence described by John seems to be in anticipation of what follows. After the 30 minutes, another angel will show up on the scene with a golden censer full of incense mixed with the prayers of God's people. As he stands at the altar before God's throne, the angel will fill the censer with fire from the altar in heaven and throw it down to earth—causing thunder, lightning, and an earthquake sent via certified mail from heaven's throne room. While the first six seal judgments relate primarily to the natural degeneration of mankind and creation, the seventh seal judgment will come directly from heaven itself.

In this scene, the prayers of God's people that have been collected will be mixed with incense and delivered to God. Then they will be mixed with heavenly fire (think judgment, power, awe) and thrown to the earth. It's as if God will be saying, "Enough is enough. I have done everything possible to offer grace, but your time is up. I will now judge the evil that my children have so often cried out for me to avenge."

God is perfectly just. He will right every wrong and must—by his nature—punish evil. God is "patient" and "not wanting anyone to perish" (2 Peter 3:9), but a time will come when his patience runs out. With the tribulation period already in full swing by this point in John's vision, the outpouring of judgment is about to be taken to a new level as God hears the cries of his own. When someone messes with your kids, all bets are off. Mama bear or papa bear comes running, and you better watch out! I believe that is—at least partly—what is depicted here. With the breaking of the seventh seal, God's abounding grace and long restraint will give way to vengeance and righteous judgment. Yet as we will see in the upcoming chapters of this book, in the midst of all this judgment God will continue to show grace to those who are willing to turn from their sinful ways and acknowledge him for who he is.

At this point the conditions depicted in John's end-time vision will go from bad to a whole lot worse. A mysterious heavenly fire will be hurled to the earth—accompanied by the staple elements of God's judgment, including thunder, lightning, and an earthquake.

QUICK FACT: DID YOU KNOW...

that the throne room in heaven is also the temple in heaven and that the earthly Jewish tabernacle and temple were patterned after it?

The Trumpet Judgments

Next we come to the trumpet judgments. The first four show up in the second part of Revelation chapter 8. Following is a brief description of what will happen.

Trumpet Judgment 1: Hail, Fire, and Blood from the Sky

When the first trumpet judgment is sounded, one-third of the vegetation and 100 percent of the earth's grass will be burned up. I've heard various natural and supernatural explanations given for the potential causes of the hail, fire, and blood, but the bottom line is that the earth will be scorched. One-third of the forests and vegetation will be destroyed, and all grass will be too.

The fact that all grass will be scorched lets us know that this will be a global catastrophe. Either the phenomenon will happen everywhere vegetation exists, or it will occur on one side of the earth (as in the case of a massive meteor shower or the effects of a coronal mass ejection from the sun), with the resulting excessive heat affecting the entire planet and destroying all grass everywhere.

Trumpet Judgment 2: Flaming "Mountain" Landing in the Ocean

With the second trumpet judgment, John depicts "something like a huge mountain, all ablaze" being thrown into the sea. John described what he saw as best he could, but most likely didn't know what an asteroid or giant meteor was. Almost 2,000 years before Bruce Willis and his crew attempted to land on and destroy an earthbound asteroid in the movie *Armageddon*, John describes one such celestial object that will land in the ocean when the second trumpet judgment occurs.

The ensuing tsunamis and devastation will destroy one-third of the life in the seas and one-third of the ships in the oceans. I took a quick look at MarineTraffic.com and, as of this writing, there are 172,277 legally registered ships larger than 65 feet in length in the oceans of our world today. That means around 57,000 large ships would be destroyed in short order by the second trumpet judgment if it were to happen today.

Trumpet Judgment 3: A Great Falling Star Poisons Water Sources

The third trumpet will bring another falling celestial object, a "great star, blazing like a torch." According to John, this projectile has a name—Wormwood. There is speculation about the nature of this "star," but it seems that Wormwood may be a nuclear weapon, or a large meteor or asteroid. Whatever it is, Wormwood will poison one-third of the world's drinking supply, causing many people to die.

While I was writing this, my college-age son was taking an elective course about the plants of the Bible. Knowing that I was working on this book, he called me one day to say his class had just studied a plant called wormwood. The plant has positive healthy applications when used in moderation, but can have deadly poisonous effects if too much is ingested. That sounds a lot like nuclear energy, doesn't it? When controlled, nuclear power can provide energy for an entire city. When released destructively, however, it can destroy a city, and the resulting radiation fallout can affect the water and environment over much larger areas. Perhaps these are clues about the nature of this "great star" that will fall after the third trumpet sounds. Or, perhaps the falling object itself will be poisonous, or it will release toxic fumes or materials upon hitting the earth.

QUICK FACT: DID YOU KNOW...

that the Ukranian city of Chernobyl (where a nuclear disaster took place in 1986) gets its name from the plant known as wormwood?

Trumpet Judgment 4: Sun, Moon, and Stars Dimmed by One-Third

The logical result of fiery meteor showers, a giant asteroid, and nuclear weapons striking the earth in quick succession would be a massive partial blackout. In addition to these direct calamities it's also possible that more earthquakes and volcanoes will be triggered by these high-powered events. As smoke and destruction rise in the air, the heavenly lights created by God to guide mankind will be dimmed to a mere two-thirds of their normal brightness. The landscape and atmosphere will take on an increasingly apocalyptic appearance.

The Talking Eagle

When I read the scene John describes in the final verse of Revelation 8, I envision it as a continuous shot from a well-crafted movie. As the camera pans across the scorched landscape then tilts upward to reveal the sun—eerily dimmed by the postapocalyptic haze—suddenly the silhouette of a bird of prey enters the frame at close range, with the bird giving a loud screech. As viewers regain their composure after almost jumping out of their skin, they realize that the screeching has an otherworldly voice-like sound to it.

The camera tracks with the bird as the lighting shifts and reveals that the bird is a large, imposing eagle. And it is speaking—like a human. With its loud, screeching voice, the eagle proclaims, "Woe! Woe! Woe to the inhabitants of the earth, because of the trumpet blasts about to be sounded by the other three angels!"

The Greek word used here for "woe" is *ouai*, an expression of grief and denunciation. It conveys the idea of long-overdue punishment or vengeance. Some Bible translations render the word "terror." That seems fitting, as we'll learn in the next chapter. If the movie clip I describe above had modern vernacular subtitles for this scene, it would read, "Look out! Y'all are in big trouble! God is about to bring it. Nowhere to run. Nowhere to hide. If you thought things were bad already, wait until you see the next three judgments! Turn to him while you can—or be destroyed."

After the first four trumpet judgments take place, an eagle will warn that the final three will be of another category. They will be even more severe with some new dimensions, as we'll see in the next chapter.

The 144,000 and Us

One lesson we can learn from the 144,000 is that we, too, are strategically placed "for such a time as this." You and I have an opportunity unlike any other generation. We are currently witnessing the fulfillment of end-times Bible prophecy. Israel is a nation again. The Jewish people are present in Jerusalem again. Many events taking place now are setting the stage for all that will occur during the end times. No one knows the day or the hour, but generations of Christians have longed to see what we are seeing right now. Let's take a cue from our future fellow-evangelists known as the 144,000 and share our faith with tactful boldness and love while there is still time.

> Esther 4:14—If you remain silent at this time, relief and deliverance for the Jews will arise from another place, but you and your father's family will perish. And who knows but that you have come to your royal position for such a time as this?

We have an opportunity to share Christ with those around us. We need to do so prayerfully and carefully, yet boldly and with a sense of urgency—much like the 144,000 Jewish evangelists who will enter the scene soon after the rapture. If we are the generation that takes part in the rapture, that means these 144,000 spoken of by John are alive today. We don't know this for certain, of course, but it is a very real possibility. My hope is this book will give you a sense of urgency and excitement as you walk with the Lord and share your faith with those around you.

If you don't know the Lord as your Savior, please settle that issue immediately. None of us is guaranteed our next breath, and there are many indications that our time on this earth is sprinting to the finish line.

CHAPTER 7

The Paranormal Becomes the New Normal

Let all who live in the land tremble, for the day of the LORD is coming. It is close at hand— a day of darkness and gloom, a day of clouds and blackness. Like dawn spreading across the mountains a large and mighty army comes, such as never was in ancient times nor ever will be in ages to come.

JOEL 2:1-2

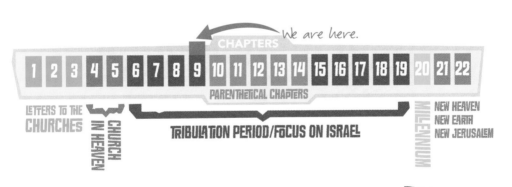

We are here.

CHAPTERS

1 2 3 4 5 6 7 8 9 10 11 12 13 14 15 16 17 18 19 20 21 22

PARENTHETICAL CHAPTERS

LETTERS TO THE CHURCHES

CHURCH IN HEAVEN

TRIBULATION PERIOD/FOCUS ON ISRAEL

MILLENNIUM

NEW HEAVEN
NEW EARTH
NEW JERUSALEM

Today we live in a time when—as believers—our faith has not yet become sight. We believe the miraculous events surrounding creation, the exodus, and those related to Jesus's birth, death, and resurrection. What we forget is that in between those shorter seasons during which the normal and paranormal intersected

WE ARE CALLED TO WALK BY FAITH WHILE WE HAVE THE OPPORTUNITY!

LITERAL INTERPRETATION EXPERT
$7 PER PROCLAMATION

FAITH'S LEMONADE
$2.00

in a major way there were longer seasons during which believers of old had to live by faith.

While miracles do still occur today, they do so on a smaller scale. I have heard too many credible stories from missionaries, Christian doctors, and believers in oppressive countries to say miracles don't occur in our day. My point is that we don't see the large-scale supernatural miracles of old. The church age is intentionally designed to be an era during which we live by faith. But with the single event of the rapture, all of that will change—forever.

The church age began with a miracle in Acts chapter 2 with the arrival of the Holy Spirit. In like fashion, the church age will end with a miracle when all believers—along with the Holy Spirit indwelling them—will miraculously exit the scene via the rapture. That single momentous event will usher in the most supernatural era since the beginning of the church.

QUICK FACT: DID YOU KNOW...

that the Holy Spirit would "come and go" in the Old Testament, but during the church age he indwells every true believer at the moment of salvation? First Corinthians 6:19 says our bodies are "temples of the Holy Spirit."

Through the seven seal judgments and the first four trumpet judgments we've seen some supernatural activity on earth, but with the arrival of the final three trumpet judgments—or woes, as the flying eagle called them—a new level of paranormal involvement will occur. It's almost as if the veil between the seen and unseen realms will be worn thinner and thinner with each wave of judgment. Some translations render the three "woes" as the three "terrors." We're about to find out why. At this point in John's vision, things are about to take a weird and wild turn. Buckle up; Revelation 9 is not for the squeamish. The next judgments described by John will—in a very real sense—release hell on earth. This is a hard truth and one of the reasons many are afraid to read the book of Revelation, but if you know Christ before that terrible time, you will escape the judgments by way of our blessed hope—the rapture!

Demonic Locusts from the Abyss

Sounds like the name of a horror movie, right? The fifth trumpet will usher in a terrifying judgment. The first 11 verses of Revelation 9 describe yet another falling "star." Unlike the previous falling objects, however, this one is given personality—it is referred to as "he" in verse 2. When I first studied this chapter, I thought this star may be Satan himself, but later in Revelation we read that Satan won't be cast down to earth until the midpoint of the tribulation. That leads me to think the star spoken of here, and seen as the leader of this demonic horde, is another high-ranking fallen angel—one of Satan's underlings.

This fallen angel will be "given the key to the shaft of the Abyss." The term "Abyss" is understood to be a temporary prison where some fallen evil entities are held (see Luke 8:30-31; 2 Peter 2:4; Jude 5-7). Whether this abyss is a physical place beneath the earth's crust or exists in the unseen realm, the "key" will unlock a barrier and release a thick, foul, sky-darkening horde of demonic "locusts." This will look like something straight out of a sci-fi movie—except it will be horribly real.

These locusts from the abyss will be given the power to hurt people with a terrible and lasting scorpion-like sting. They will be led by a fallen angel named Destroyer (*Abaddon* in Hebrew, or *Apollyon* in Greek). I'm not sure if this being is the star who fell to earth with the key to the abyss, or whether he is a different fallen angel—the one currently ruling over the abyss and its horde of locust-demons. Joel chapter 2 also describes these terrible creatures that will invade earth during the tribulation period.

We often think of angels and fallen angels as being ghost-like spirits with no physicality, but a careful review of angelology (the study of angels) reveals some truly interesting insights—not the least of which is the fact that angels can take on physical attributes. As we noted earlier, the deeper we go into the tribulation period, the more the seen and the unseen realms will intersect with greater frequency and intensity. That is foreign to us in our day, but it's what will happen as the tribulation period unfolds.

QUICK FACT: DID YOU KNOW...

that CERN is the world's biggest machine, is buried underground, has the Hindu god Shiva (aka "the Destroyer") as its mascot, uses a logo with three sixes worked into the design, is partially located in the area where ancient Romans had a temple to the god Apollo (see Apollyon referenced in Revelation 9:11), and has among its goals to open a portal to other dimensions and to tap into "dark matter"? Coincidence or foreshadow?[1]

Four Killer Angels and the Demonic 200-Million-Man Army

As if the fifth trumpet (the first woe) wasn't crazy enough, the sixth trumpet (the second woe) surely will be. Apparently, right now there are fallen angels bound in chains (you can read about this in the book of Jude and a few other places in Scripture) and reserved for a certain day and purpose. Here in Revelation 9:13 and following, John tells us about four such angels—bound at the Euphrates River. It is interesting to me that the river has kept its name since the book of Genesis, and we know its location even today.

These four fallen angels will lead a demonic horde of 200 million soldiers to kill one-third of those alive on earth at that time. Keep in mind that many people will have already died during the previous judgments—particularly the fourth seal judgment, when war, famine, and disease will have killed one-fourth of the world's population (Revelation 6:8). By the end of the sixth trumpet judgment, more than half of the world's population will have been killed. Today there are almost 7.8 billion people living on earth.[2] If the tribulation were to start now, that means almost 2 billion would die during the fourth seal judgment and almost 2 billion more during the sixth trumpet judgment. Horrific!

Bible prophecy experts offer two main views regarding this future army. Some say the text is describing the same army we find later in Revelation 16, brought together by the "kings of the east," who will cross the dried-up Euphrates River as they march toward Israel and the final tribulation-era battle, the Armageddon campaign. Others say this seems to be a demonic army—a larger-scale force than the demonic locusts released from the abyss during the fifth trumpet judgment.

Perhaps it is a hybrid of the two. As I mentioned, this will be a time when the normal and the paranormal mix like never before. It could be that China or another Asian entity with a large population develops a demonic hybrid army of creatures. It is widely known that the militaries of several countries around the world—most notably China—have been experimenting with DNA splicing to create super-soldiers and other chimera-like creatures. For example, scientists have already begun to breed "super-dogs" that have twice the muscle of a normal dog, and they have been editing human genes since at least 2015.[3]

There is also a vast and growing secular movement known as transhumanism—people who believe in self-guided "evolution" using emerging genetic and cybernetic technologies. The leaders of this movement are trying to achieve eternal life (apart from God) through integrating technology with the human species. It is the merging of man and machine.[4]

Going back to the 200-million-man army—John describes the members of this army as riding horse-like creatures with lion-like heads that launch fire, weaponized snake-like tails, and bright, colorful armor of red, blue, and yellow. For all we know, the "horses" described by  John could be some type of demonic weaponized chimera, or John's attempt to describe the weaponry that will be used in the future.

Add to our current knowledge of super-soldier programs and the transhumanism movement the fact that during the tribulation period, evil will be fully embraced. Revelation informs us that evil rulers and their unbelieving subjects will openly practice sorcery, witchcraft, and demonic worship. They will partner with demonic entities to devise plans like the world has never seen. It is widely known that Hitler and the Nazis were steeped in occult practices. Now, imagine a time much worse than that, led by a ruler much more wicked and powerful than Hitler—a ruler who has technology far superior to anything that has ever existed. Whatever the nature of this 200-million-man army, it will be unlike anything the world has ever seen.

QUICK FACT: DID YOU KNOW...

that militaries around the world are creating weaponized robot animals for use in battle?[5]

Man's Response

The truly amazing thing about the sixth trumpet judgment is not the strange future-tech chimeras or the gigantic size of the army, but man's lack of repentance after witnessing all this. Today, the grey is fading. People and movements are polarizing and picking distinct sides. More and more we find that the truths and values of Scripture are either loved or hated. With each passing year, there is less common ground between those who have differing views.

During the tribulation period, this dynamic will escalate with each judgment. Though many will turn to the Lord after the shock of the rapture and through the ministries of the 144,000 evangelists, many others will harden their hearts. This is especially true toward the end of the tribulation. In Revelation 9:20-21 we read,

> The rest of mankind who were not killed by these plagues still did not repent of the work of their hands; they did not stop worshiping demons, and idols of gold, silver, bronze, stone and wood—idols that cannot see or hear or walk. Nor did they repent of their murders, their magic arts, their sexual immorality or their thefts.

Notice that even during God's judgment, repentance is still an option. God's grace is always present with his judgment. Yet there will come a point of no return, when grace and forgiveness are no longer extended. But until that moment, God's undeserved favor is still available to all. The sad fact is that each time a person rejects the offer, his or her heart grows harder toward it.

As we'll see in the upcoming chapters, this hard-heartedness and rebellion will escalate into all-out war against God. A foolish proposition to be sure, but evil will be so rampant and deception so thorough that man will rage against God like an ant that thinks it could take on a silverback gorilla.

This is a practical reminder to us to respond to God when his path intersects ours. These are defining moments that give us the opportunity to experience God and grow in his ways. If you don't know the Lord, please respond to his offer of salvation. If you are a believer, determine today to live for the things of God that you don't yet see. The invasion of the seen realm by the unseen realm continues in the next chapter of Revelation, where we'll meet a giant angel with a mysterious little book.

CHAPTER 8

A Giant Roaring Angel

I saw another mighty angel coming down from heaven. He was robed in a cloud, with a rainbow above his head; his face was like the sun, and his legs were like fiery pillars. He was holding a little scroll, which lay open in his hand. He planted his right foot on the sea and his left foot on the land, and he gave a loud shout like the roar of a lion.

REVELATION 10:1-3

We are here.

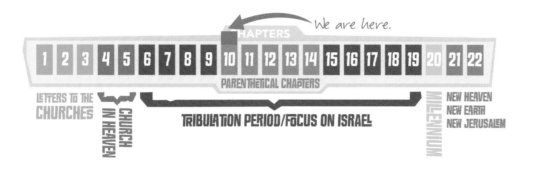

CHAPTERS

| 1 | 2 | 3 | 4 | 5 | 6 | 7 | 8 | 9 | 10 | 11 | 12 | 13 | 14 | 15 | 16 | 17 | 18 | 19 | 20 | 21 | 22 |

PARENTHETICAL CHAPTERS

LETTERS TO THE CHURCHES

CHURCH IN HEAVEN

TRIBULATION PERIOD/FOCUS ON ISRAEL

MILLENNIUM

NEW HEAVEN
NEW EARTH
NEW JERUSALEM

In my early twenties I took a few audit classes at a nearby Bible college and at my local church, which was an extension site. While I have never felt called to go to Bible college or seminary, I had a desire to learn more. One of the classes I took was an overview of the book of Revelation, which, up to that time, had confused me. I had a hard time separating symbols from literal events, and I didn't see how anyone could make real sense of the book.

One day in class we were discussing symbolism as we dissected Revelation 10, and I asked the professor, "What do you think this giant angel standing on earth represents?" His simple yet profound answer surprised me. He replied, "A giant angel standing on the earth." He wasn't trying to be funny; he was reinforcing the foundational principles he had already taught at the beginning of the course but I had yet to fully grasp—that we should use a literal approach to interpretation to understand prophecy and Scripture. This was a key moment in my pursuit to unravel Revelation, and it eventually unlocked a much fuller understanding of the book for me.

Wherever symbolism is used, the meaning of the symbol is either found in the immediate context or elsewhere in Scripture. In the Bible, the first mention of a symbol is particularly important. Taking the time to do cross-reference studies of symbolism in the Bible is fascinating and eye-opening. As I mentioned earlier, there are more than 800 references to the Old Testament in Revelation—many of which are symbols that point back to the original context.

If you use the literal, futurist interpretation method to study Revelation, the book isn't all that difficult to understand—but it may be hard to believe. You and I have never seen Jesus in all his glory with our physical eyes. We've never seen a literal, gigantic, Godzilla-dwarfing angel standing on the earth and towering into the stratosphere. But that doesn't mean it won't happen. If you and I believe the first verse of the Bible, then nothing else in Scripture should be difficult to believe.

Those ten simple words—"In the beginning God created the heavens and the earth" (Genesis 1:1)—are more unbelievable than anything else in Scripture. Yet they must be true logically. If anything exists, something or someone has to be eternal—because something can't come from nothing. Or to put it another way—if ever there was a time when nothing existed, then nothing could exist now. When applying logic to the world around us, we know intuitively that something has to be eternal and that something had to be the first cause of time, space, and matter as we know it.

QUICK FACT: DID YOU KNOW...
that the logical need for a first cause is known as the Cosmological Argument?

If we know the first cause is a logical fact, and if we believe the biblical account of how creation occurred, none of the supernatural events in Revelation should throw us for a loop. Are they foreign, weird, strange, and fantastical? Absolutely. And this is only the tip of the iceberg. But if we believe God created everything out of nothing, then nothing else Scripture says should be difficult for us to believe.

When we use the literal interpretation method and allow Scripture to provide its own meaning for the symbols and figures of speech that appear within its pages, we will be able to understand Revelation like never before. It is helpful to realize that John was describing a future time when supernatural events will once again be global in scale and regular in occurrence. God will not bring about final judgment without first making people choose clear sides. The tribulation period will demonstrate that even when people are given all the physical proof they need for belief in God, many will still choose to openly and stubbornly rebel against their creator.

The Lion Roars

Here in the opening verses of Revelation 10 we bump into this "mighty angel"—the largest, most magnificent angel yet. In the Bible we discover that there are different types of angels. Some look like animals; others look like humans. We find various categories and ranks of angels. Scripture even indicates that Christians have some type of guardian angels (Matthew 18:10). We don't know if they use man-to-man or zone defense, but they are involved in the life of every believer, helping God work out his plans behind the scenes.

Angels can take on human form with physical bodies, as seen in the case of the rescue of Lot (Genesis 19:1-29). Angels are associated with stars (Isaiah 14:12) and are referred to as the "sons of God" (Job 1:6)—as in the direct creations of God. Just as there are multitudes of animal kinds in all varieties, we see this same creative beauty and diversity in the unseen realm as well. Angels come in all shapes, sizes, and ranks.

Among the various accounts of angels in Scripture, we find several descriptions in the Old Testament of an important and mysterious figure known as the Angel of the Lord, or "the commander of the army of the LORD" (Joshua 5:13-15). Given Revelation's significant connection to the Old Testament, it makes complete sense for this mysterious figure to show up again during the tribulation period.

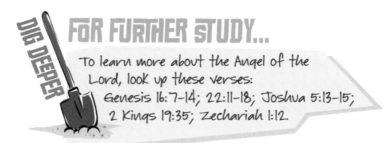

FOR FURTHER STUDY...

To learn more about the Angel of the Lord, look up these verses:
Genesis 16:7-14; 22:11-18; Joshua 5:13-15; 2 Kings 19:35; Zechariah 1:12.

In Scripture, the word translated *angel* means "messenger." Many Bible scholars say that the accounts of the Angel of the Lord, the commander of the Lord's army, and other descriptions of God showing up in human form are preincarnate (before he was born in the manger) appearances of Jesus (see John 1:1-3,14). Some also believe this spectacular angel described in Revelation 10 is Jesus appearing in glorified form. Not all prophecy experts agree on this, but the specific details about this angel and a careful comparison with John's vision of Jesus in Revelation 1 indicate this figure may very well be the risen, glorified, earth-reclaiming Christ. I believe this is likely the case, but I'm not dogmatic about it. It could just be another magnificent angel—a proxy for the Lord, so to speak.

Clouds, rainbows, a face of blinding glory, and glowing legs are details mentioned in John's vision of Christ in Revelation 1 and in the throne room of heaven in Revelation 4. Also, don't miss the fact that the angel roars like a lion, and Jesus is "the Lion of the tribe of Judah" (Revelation 5:5). So what exactly is going on here?

Lions roar to let everyone in hearing distance know that they are in the lion's territory. It's how lions claim their space. I have heard lions roar at the National Zoo in Washington, DC. Their roars are absolutely awe-inspiring and can be heard for miles. The roar mentioned in Revelation 10:3 will be the roar heard around the world.

I believe the angel in Revelation 10 is very likely Jesus standing on land and sea and towering into the sky (symbolic of all creation, see verse 6), voicing a roar that will be heard around the world. With this action he will essentially be saying, "I, the Son, was alone worthy to open the title deed to earth. Now I'm here to reclaim all land, sea, and sky for the Father— and everyone who can hear my voice had better pay attention!"

QUICK FACT: DID YOU NOTICE...

that the figure is standing "on" the sea, not "in" the sea?
Who else can you think of in the Bible who walked on water?

The Seven Thunders

Immediately after the earth-vibrating roar, we read this in Revelation 10:3-4: "When he shouted, the voices of the seven thunders spoke. And when the seven thunders spoke, I was about to write; but I heard a voice from heaven say, 'Seal up what the seven thunders have said and do not write it down.'"

Perhaps the seven thunders are seven proclamations of judgment from God. Each time we read about thunder in Revelation, it comes from the throne room of God or is associated with God's voice. In God's throne room, the Holy Spirit is seen as the seven spirits of God (remember that seven is the number of fullness or completion). The statements from the seven thunders of God are the only proclamations from the book of Revelation that remain sealed. Perhaps these details about God's judgment were too horrific or terrifying to record. The use of the number seven indicates some type of finality, fullness, or completion—which fits logically with the statement in this passage (dealt with below) about the mystery of God being accomplished.

FOR FURTHER STUDY...

DIG DEEPER

God's thunderous voice:
1 Samuel 2:10; 2 Samuel 22:14;
Psalm 18:13

No More Delay

Adding further weight to the importance of Revelation chapter 10 is the statement by the angel that there would be "no more delay." After the lion roar and the seven thunders, the giant angel positions himself to take a solemn oath. We read in Revelation 10:5-6, "The angel I had seen standing on the sea and on the land raised his right hand to heaven. And he swore by him who lives for ever and ever, who created the heavens and all that is in them, the earth and all that is in it, and the sea and all that is in it, and said, 'There will be no more delay!'"

The message here is clear. At this point during the tribulation period, God will essentially say, "Enough messing around. No more waiting. It's time to put the final set of judgments in motion." This mysterious and pivotal set of events is clearly an important turning point in God's end-time plan and in the book of Revelation.

Mystery

In the Bible, a mystery is something that is unknown unless (and until) revealed by God. There are several New Testament mystery doctrines—teachings that are concealed in the Old Testament and revealed in the New. Not until after the mysteries are unveiled can they be seen hidden in plain sight in the Old Testament. Examples include the mysteries of the gospel (Romans 16:25), the rapture (1 Corinthians 15:51-53), Jesus (Colossians 2:2-3), and the church (Ephesians 5:32).

Moving on to Revelation 10:7, we read, "In the days when the seventh angel is about to sound his trumpet, the mystery of God will be accomplished, just as he announced to his servants the prophets." Coupled with the statement earlier about there being no more delay, this key detail affirms that we have arrived at a monumental moment. The dramatic scene described above is the prelude to the final trumpet judgment, which will be a game changer in terms of fulfilling or accomplishing a specific mystery of God.

The Greek word used here for "be accomplished" is *tetelestai*. It comes from the same root word (*telos*) that Jesus used in John 19:30 when he was on the cross and cried out, "It is finished." This term carries with it the connotation that the event in question is complete, fulfilled, and brought to an end. We also know from Colossians 2:2-3 that the mystery of God is Jesus. In God's eyes, the complete mystery of Jesus and all related prophecies at this point during the tribulation period are a done deal. There's still half of the tribulation to go, but the midpoint of the tribulation period will be a point of no return.

Before the seventh trumpet is blown, the remainder of all unfulfilled prophecies related to Jesus and the culmination of all things will be as good as done. The punishment of the nations, the casting of the beast and false prophet into Lake of Fire, the establishment of Christ's kingdom, the refurbishing of the earth, the church ruling and reigning with Christ for 1,000 years, the arrival of the New Jerusalem, the banishing of Satan into the Lake of Fire forever, the great white throne judgment, the new heavens and the new earth—all of these will be as good as done. God will finally respond fully to the question of evil. He will take revenge for every innocent ever wronged.

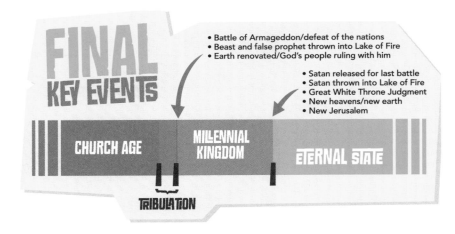

FINAL KEY EVENTS

- Battle of Armageddon/defeat of the nations
- Beast and false prophet thrown into Lake of Fire
- Earth renovated/God's people ruling with him

- Satan released for last battle
- Satan thrown into Lake of Fire
- Great White Throne Judgment
- New heavens/new earth
- New Jerusalem

CHURCH AGE | MILLENNIAL KINGDOM | ETERNAL STATE

TRIBULATION

The Little Scroll

There's one more important detail to note in Revelation 10—John scarfing down a sweet-tasting scroll, then getting an instantaneous stomach bug (verses 8-10). Bible scholars say the little scroll is God's Word—the Bible. It is a love letter—

a sweet book of grace, forgiveness, wholeness, reconciliation, and restoration. But it also reminds us that there will be judgment, destruction, and separation for those who reject God's clear and loving offer of grace. At this point in John's vision, the second half of the tribulation is about to begin—and everything is about to get as bad as ever. John was told (while he's in a heap on the floor trying to keep his act together) that he must prophesy again to many people. Though God's Word was sweet, John was about to be given the difficult job of bearing bad news to his people and the world.

The Old Testament prophet Ezekiel was given

a similar command (Ezekiel 2:9–3:3)—he was instructed to eat a scroll that was sweet like honey. In that passage, God's message given to Ezekiel was also compared to honey as he ate the scroll. We find this same symbolism in Psalm 19:9-10 as well: "The decrees of the LORD are firm, and all of them are righteous. They are more precious than gold, than much pure gold; they are sweeter than honey."

Our Stomachache

We can relate to John's strange, delicious meal—and his sour stomach. As we meditate on God's Word, study it, and imperfectly attempt to live it out in real life, it is sweet and fulfilling. The more we study and apply the Bible, the more its teachings become a part of us. As we experience all this, we find ourselves wishing that we could somehow translate that belief to others who have never experienced the Bible's beauty, truth, and life-changing effects.

At the same time, we may find that we have a pain in the depths of our souls as we think of the billions who will miss the rapture, or worse yet, spend eternity apart from God's presence. This pain is never more intense than when we think of friends and loved ones who—for whatever reason—can't seem to see the truth of God's Word or their need for a Savior.

Romans 1:20—Since the creation of the world God's invisible qualities—his eternal power and divine nature—have been clearly seen, being understood from what has been made, so that people are without excuse.

If the concept of hell seems too harsh to our fallen human sensibilities, it's only because we can't fully see the depth of our own sin or the lengths God went to make it possible for us to avoid eternal punishment. Hell is not a torture chamber created by a cruel, sadistic creator. Rather, it is a necessary spiritual reality created originally for Satan and the fallen angels (Matthew 25:41). When we struggle with the reality of hell, we need to realize that (1) we don't have all knowledge, and (2) God is completely just. Sin and holiness can't coexist side by side, and all wrongs must eventually be made right.

The descriptions of hell, as given in the Bible, are the best way the Holy Spirit could describe what life will be like for someone who is completely removed from God's presence. Hell is referred to in some Bible passages as "outer darkness." Life apart from God will be dark, hopeless, cold, and painful. We see that on a small scale now as we witness people trying to fill the void within themselves with pleasure, comfort, possessions, or power—only to find the emptiness remains. Now imagine that separation and emptiness pushed to its fullest possible form.

Matthew 11:28-29—Come to me, all you who are weary and burdened, and I will give you rest. Take my yoke upon you and learn from me, for I am gentle and humble in heart, and you will find rest for your souls.

The fact hell is real—and that Christ is returning soon—should drive us to tell others about the good news that God has done everything possible to reconcile them to him so they can bask in his presence forever. The alternative is terrible and real—and unnecessary. You and I have the sweetest, richest, life-giving message. Let's commit to sharing this message with tact and respect while we still have time. We just might be able to minimize our stomachache a bit as we see people being reconciled with God through the Lord Jesus Christ.

One day relatively soon, the Lamb slain from the foundation of the world will roar like a lion and the Savior will come to reclaim the territory that was stolen from him. Let's live for that day and do our best to take people to heaven with us by the truckloads.

CHAPTER 9

The Tipping Point

He will confirm a covenant with many for one "seven." In the middle of the "seven" he will put an end to sacrifice and offering. And at the temple he will set up an abomination that causes desolation, until the end that is decreed is poured out on him.

DANIEL 9:27

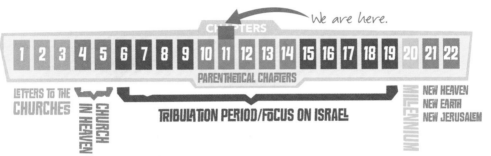

We are here.

CHAPTERS

1 2 3 4 5 6 7 8 9 10 11 12 13 14 15 16 17 18 19 20 21 22

PARENTHETICAL CHAPTERS

LETTERS TO THE CHURCHES

CHURCH IN HEAVEN

TRIBULATION PERIOD/FOCUS ON ISRAEL

MILLENNIUM

NEW HEAVEN
NEW EARTH
NEW JERUSALEM

A couple summers ago, my family and I went to Hershey Park in Hershey, Pennsylvania, to meet with some family and let all the cousins hang out together. In addition to eating too much chocolate, I discovered a new generation of roller coasters that have rocket-like takeoff speeds and over-the-top heights with insane drop angles.

Those roller coasters provided an intense thrill ride, but I still have great nostalgia for the old-school wooden roller coasters

that bang your ribs around and almost throw you from the car. There's something about that slow climb up the first big hill and the increasing anticipation and heart rate that comes with each tick, tick, tick of the mechanical pulley system. The excitement builds as you get to the top—and you know you're at the tipping point where there's no turning back from the wild ride that is about to commence. You have a brief moment to take in the sights as you view the landscape below and notice that you can see for what seems like 100 miles. Just then gravity takes over, your stomach drops, and your grip tightens on whatever your hands can grab onto for stability. You are now at the mercy of the ride.

Well, that's where we are at this point in our study of Revelation. We're at the top of the highest point on the track, where all the setup is complete and momentum is about to take over. This is the point of no return, a point at which the roller-coaster cars are about to fall and there's no stopping them. At this juncture, God's kingdom and the culmination of all things will have all but arrived.

Midpoint

Similar to an old-school roller coaster, chapters 10–14 are parenthetical in nature and give us a brief moment to survey the landscape to get more context. Up till now in Revelation we've been viewing individual sequential events at ground level. But now we are taken high above the seven-year tribulation period to view the broader context that will help us understand the key events that will occur at the midpoint of the tribulation.

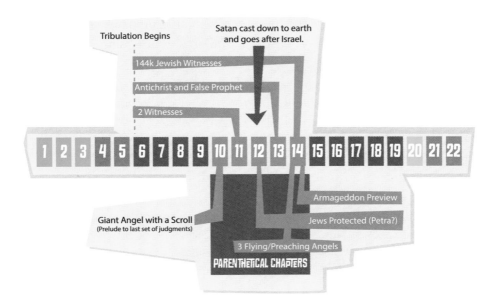

We understand from prophecies in the book of Daniel that the tribulation is a seven-year long period (Daniel 9). It will begin when the figure known as the antichrist enforces a seven-year treaty between Israel and "many." We also know from the book of Daniel and Jesus's Olivet Discourse (Matthew 24–25) that at the exact midpoint of the seven-year period the "abomination of desolation" will occur. Revelation chapters 10–14 provide the fuller context of the events related to the midpoint of the tribulation. As we'll find out in Revelation 11–14, there are several other key events that take place at the midpoint, and we'll unpack each one as it is presented in those chapters.

Temple Talk

In the opening verses of Revelation 11, John is given instructions to measure the temple. He is told to "exclude the outer court…because it has been given to the Gentiles." Then he is told that the Gentiles will "trample on the

TEN KEY MID-TRIB EVENTS

1. Antichrist killed
2. Satan cast down to Earth
3. Antichrist "resurrected"
4. Religious Babylon destroyed
5. Abomination of Desolation
6. Covenant broken
7. Jews persecuted worldwide
8. Mark of the beast implemented
9. Worship of antichrist
10. 2 witnesses killed

holy city for 42 months." This comes out to 3.5 years—the first half of the tribulation period.

The city in view here is Jerusalem, and the temple spoken of is the future third Jewish temple. Solomon's temple was the first, and it was destroyed in 587 BC by Nebuchadnezzar. The second temple was built on the same location when the Jewish people returned to their land after the 70-year Babylonian captivity. Later, during the reign of Herod, this same temple was overhauled and became part of a vast temple complex. Because of that, it became known as Herod's temple. This second temple was destroyed in AD 70 by the Roman legions led by Titus.

This brings us to the third temple, which has yet to be rebuilt. The last four verses of Daniel 9 give us key event markers for the Jewish people from Daniel's time to the end. Beginning with a command to rebuild the second temple (recorded in Nehemiah), Daniel 9 gives us key prophecies about Jesus's first coming as well as a last days' seven-year span of time that we now know is the tribulation period. We are told in Daniel 9:27 about an end-time ruler, his seven-year covenant with Israel (which seems to include the rebuilding of a third temple), and a key mid-tribulation event known (and spoken of by Jesus in Matthew 24:15) as the abomination of desolation. Paul also mentions a future third temple in 2 Thessalonians 2:4.

Though not explicitly stated anywhere in Scripture, it seems that the building of the third temple will be part of the seven-year covenant. Notice that Daniel 9:27 says the antichrist will "confirm" a covenant. The Hebrew word used there means to "make it strong." Some translations render it "enforce" or "strengthen." This seems to suggest that the antichrist is going to strengthen and enforce an existing treaty that has already been on the table.

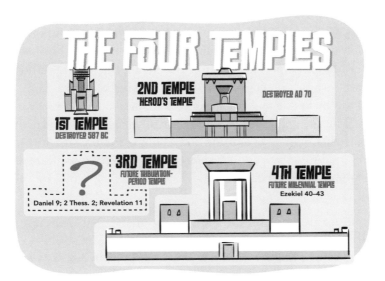

When Israel miraculously became a nation again in 1948, it was immediately attacked on all sides by Arab enemies. With untrained soldiers, few weapons, and all odds stacked against her, Israel survived. In 1967, she was attacked again by an even greater number of Arab enemies, yet amazingly she defeated them all in six days and regained control of Jerusalem. For the first time since 587 BC, the Jewish people were in sovereign control of Jerusalem again. But due to the Muslim holy sites (Al-Aqsa Mosque and the Dome of the Rock) that had been built on the Temple Mount, Israel—in an attempt to establish peace—graciously gave control of the Temple Mount to Muslim authorities. This arrangement continues to this day.

If you think about it, that is a strange set of circumstances. Israel regained her ancient city and historic holy site, but in her secular rebirth (prophesied in Ezekiel 36–37), she gave up control of the very Temple Mount that originally belonged to her. This is where things get interesting with regard to Revelation 11.

I believe that the treaty that will be strengthened and confirmed by the antichrist will be a final version of the many iterations of a peace agreement which has been proposed by every United States president since Nixon in 1977. Each president has developed, reformatted, and pushed for a Mid-East peace treaty with none other than Israel and Jerusalem at its center.

There are competing views about where the temple originally stood on the Temple Mount complex. Some say the Dome of the Rock is built in the area of the outer court, while others say it is built directly on the site where the temple—and possibly the inner rooms (including the Holy of Holies)—once stood. This is a matter I have not personally studied in depth, but several authors I trust (some of whom are archeologists) make a very strong case for the latter view. In my mind this makes sense theologically. Satan, in his age-old attempt to keep prophecy from being fulfilled, would surely do his best to have anything but the temple built on the exact location of the Holy of Holies. He is a usurper and has always tried to replace and counterfeit God at every turn. If he thinks he can keep prophecy from being fulfilled, he will influence people by any means necessary to make that so.

In any case, at this moment, the Temple Institute in Israel currently has produced all the utensils, priestly garments, construction plans, and a groundswell of support to build a third temple. They are fully ready to reinstitute animal sacrifices and all the functions needed for the temple to operate again. The recently formed Sanhedrin (which has not existed since AD 70 when the temple was destroyed) dedicated the altar for the third temple in Jerusalem on the last day of Hanukkah in 2018. Who could have predicted that all this preparation would be in place (along with an increasing desire to build the third temple) at the same time that all other end-time conditions are converging? Only God.

The Two Fire-Breathing Witnesses

In Revelation 11, along with the references to a third temple that must be built and functional by the halfway point of the future tribulation period, we discover two strange end-time figures known as the two witnesses. They are also called the two olive trees and the two lampstands. We discover a veiled reference to these individuals in Zechariah 4:11-14, where Zechariah pushed for an answer as to who they were. He didn't get a full answer—only confirmation that they were indeed two individuals. Revelation 11:4 is a direct reference to Zechariah

4:14. Both passages reference the lampstands, olive trees, and state that these figures "stand before the Lord of the earth" (Revelation 11:4).

We are told that the two witnesses will prophesy for 1,260 days—which comes out to 3.5 years (using Israel's 360-day year model). We are told that they can breathe fire and destroy people who try to harm them, prevent rain from falling, turn water into blood, and strike the earth "with every kind of plague as often as they want" (verse 6). These end-time superheroes will undoubtedly capture the attention of the world.

At the midpoint of the tribulation, the two witnesses will be killed by the antichrist (referred to here as the beast)—to everyone's surprise and delight. In verses 9-10 we read, "For three and a half days some from every people, tribe, language and nation will gaze on their bodies and refuse them burial. The inhabitants of the earth will gloat over them and will celebrate by sending each other gifts, because these two prophets had tormented those who live on the earth."

When John wrote this, it was impossible for an event in Jerusalem to be shown around the world in real time. But today we have satellite broadcasting and smart phones in our pockets, which means we have access to real-time breaking news as it happens. That this technology currently exists lets us know we are drawing nearer to these events.

SIGNIFICANT TECHNOLOGY DATES

1962 — First Satellite TV

1980 — First 24-hour news channel

1992 — First smart phone

2000 — First camera phone

2015 — First livestreaming phone apps

2016 — Facebook Live made available[1]

Holiday Interrupted

Upon hearing that the two witnesses have died, the world will erupt into joy and initiate a new holiday tradition. They will celebrate by sending gifts to one another to commemorate the antichrist's victory over these two disruptive fire-breathing preachers. But, just as the global celebrations get into full swing, God will throw a resurrection-sized monkey wrench into the partying.

As was the case with the resurrection of Christ, this future resurrection of the two witnesses will surprise the enemy. The world will learn that what they thought was a victory will, in reality, be a back-breaking defeat. In Revelation 11:11-13 we read,

> After the three and a half days the breath of life from God entered them, and they stood on their feet, and terror struck those who saw them. Then they heard a loud voice from heaven saying to them, "Come up here." And they went up to heaven in a cloud, while their enemies looked on. At that very hour there was a severe earthquake and a tenth of the city collapsed. Seven thousand people were killed in the earthquake, and the survivors were terrified and gave glory to the God of heaven.

The ascension of the two witnesses will be reminiscent of the rapture of the church, which will have taken place 3.5 years earlier (see 1 Thessalonians 4:16-17; 2 Thessalonians 2; and 1 Corinthians 15:51-53).

Who Are They?

Many people have wondered about the identity of the two witnesses. I believe they are Moses and Elijah, and here's why: Those two key Old Testament figures traditionally represent the law and the prophets (that is, the Old Testament). As I've pointed out, the tribulation period is distinctly Jewish in focus. Moses and Elijah were also the two who showed up in Matthew 17 when Jesus was momentarily changed into his glorified body in front of Peter, James, and John.

In Matthew 17:1-3 we read,

> After six days Jesus took with him Peter, James and John the brother of James, and led them up a high mountain by themselves. There he was transfigured before them. His face shone like the sun, and his clothes became as white as the light. Just then there appeared before them Moses and Elijah, talking with Jesus.

In addition, the miraculous signs the two witnesses will perform happen to mirror those of Moses and Elijah. Also, both Moses and Elijah exited the scene in the Old Testament in unique ways. Moses died and was buried by God himself (Deuteronomy 34) under mysterious circumstances. In fact, at some point, Satan attempted to take the body of Moses (Jude 9). Elijah, on the other hand, never died. He was taken up to heaven via a tornado-driven team of fiery horses (2 Kings 2:11-12). An argument could be made that because Moses died and Elijah didn't, they represent how the law has been fulfilled or completed (Moses), but prophecy has not yet been fully fulfilled (Elijah).

Not all prophecy experts agree that the two witnesses will be Moses and Elijah, or even that they will be men who have already lived on Earth. Other popular candidates include John (the writer of Revelation) and Enoch.

The ministry of the two witnesses will likely begin after the rapture, and Revelation 11 describes what will happen to the two individuals at the midpoint of the tribulation. There is a prophecy in Malachi 4:5-6 that states, "See, I will send the prophet Elijah to you *before that great and dreadful day of the LORD* [the tribulation period] comes. He will turn the hearts of the parents to their children, and the hearts of the children to their parents; or else *I will come and strike the land with total destruction*" (emphasis added).

Based on this prophecy and the details described above, it appears that Elijah will most likely show up on the scene just after the rapture, but before the official beginning of the tribulation period—before the antichrist is revealed by virtue of enforcing Israel's "covenant with many." John the baptizer came *in the spirit and power of Elijah* (Luke 1:17) before Jesus's first-coming ministry began, but Elijah himself will enter the scene in the end times just before the tribulation period begins. Jesus affirmed this twofold fulfillment of Elijah's end-time ministry in Matthew 17:10-13.

Finally—the Seventh Trumpet

After all the buildup beginning in Revelation 10 and earlier, we reach the seventh trumpet judgment in Revelation 11:15. Unlike the other trumpets, this one does not introduce an instant calamity. As was the case with the seventh seal judgment, the seventh trumpet will serve as a prelude to the next set of judgments.

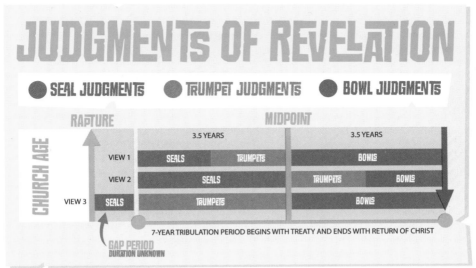

JUDGMENTS OF REVELATION

● SEAL JUDGMENTS ● TRUMPET JUDGMENTS ● BOWL JUDGMENTS

	RAPTURE		MIDPOINT	
		3.5 YEARS		3.5 YEARS
CHURCH AGE	VIEW 1	SEALS TRUMPETS		BOWLS
	VIEW 2	SEALS		TRUMPETS BOWLS
	VIEW 3	SEALS TRUMPETS		BOWLS

7-YEAR TRIBULATION PERIOD BEGINS WITH TREATY AND ENDS WITH RETURN OF CHRIST

GAP PERIOD
DURATION UNKNOWN

The three main views of tribulation events. I lean (though not dogmatically) toward VIEW 1.

As you'll recall, the seventh and final seal judgment led to 30 minutes of silence in heaven followed by the prayers of God's people being presented to the Lord. The prayers were mixed with heavenly fire then hurled down to earth along with the signature signs of God's judgment—thunder, lightning, and an earthquake.

Here in Revelation 11, with the seventh trumpet judgment, John describes the finality that will result from the series of bowl judgments that the seventh trumpet unlocks. In other words, the seventh trumpet's main purpose will be to usher in the final phase of the tribulation.

In Revelation 11:15-18, John used language that describes the ultimate result of the seven bowl judgments. For exam-

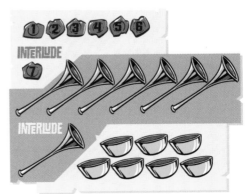

ple, in verse 15 we read, "The seventh angel sounded his trumpet, and there were loud voices in heaven, which said: 'The kingdom of the world has become the kingdom of our Lord and of his Messiah, and he will reign for ever and ever.'"

While there is still an entire half of the tribulation period to go, the seventh trumpet will unlock the seven bowl judgments, which will fully accomplish all that God prophesied for the final phase of history. God's sovereign plan—even now—is as good as done. The enemy can throw temper tantrums and lead mankind to rebellion, but absolutely nothing can stop what God has determined to do.

Finders of the Lost Ark

In the final verse of Revelation 11, we read a curious detail that is easy to overlook. Verse 19 says, "Then God's temple in heaven was opened, and within his temple was seen the ark of his covenant. And there came flashes of lightning, rumblings, peals of thunder, an earthquake and a severe hailstorm."

We've read about lightning, thunder, and earthquakes in connection with the earlier judgments. But here we see something different—the ark of the covenant appearing in God's temple in heaven!

Why is this so interesting? Up to this point in Scripture, the ark of the covenant has not been mentioned since King Josiah had it returned to the temple in Jerusalem (2 Chronicles 35:1-3; see also 2 Kings 23:21-23) at around 650 BC—about 40 years before the Babylon army conquered the Jewish people and took them into captivity in 606 BC.

No post-captivity mention of the ark is made even though we discover in the book of Daniel that other temple instruments were stolen and taken to Babylon (Daniel 5:1-4). Surely, if the ark had been taken to Babylon, Daniel would have mentioned it.

So the ark has been missing all this time. Where is it? Many speculate that it was hidden by the temple priests prior to the Babylonian captivitiy. The priests had hidden the ark once before when the temple was raided during an attack by Egypt. Later the ark was returned, but it wasn't mentioned as being among the spoils taken during the Babylonian conquest—which likely means it was hidden again.

All kinds of theories and stories have arisen about the location of the ark—some that are viable, and some that are far-fetched. The most logical that I've heard are that it was hidden beneath the temple in a secret place designed for preservation in case of an invasion, or that it was hidden offsite in an extremely remote location.

This is speculation, but what if the ark is hidden underneath the Temple Mount in a secret place designed to protect it? Because Muslim authorities control the Temple Mount, no excavating is allowed at the site. Is it possible that God is using the prevailing geopolitical dynamics to keep the location of the ark hidden until just the right time? Perhaps the covenant that will be "strengthened" by the antichrist will allow for the construction of the temple and for archeological searches to find the ark beneath the Temple Mount.

Whatever the case, Revelation 11 ends with the curious verse about the ark being in heaven at the midpoint of the tribulation period. This is no small detail. Perhaps John saw the heavenly version of the ark—Scripture tells us that the tabernacle and its furnishings were a shadow or figure that pointed to the heavenly equivalents (Hebrews 8:5).

But maybe, just maybe, the ark John mentions is the ark that formerly resided in the first temple. It was definitely a mysterious and miraculous object. In the Old Testament we discover that the ark had the power to kill those who handled it carelessly. It also preserved Aaron's flowering staff and some manna that would normally rot after one day. The ark is a supernatural vault in which time stands still and decay cannot occur. It also carried the stone tablets on which God himself wrote the Ten Commandments with his own rock-melting "finger."

Clearly, the ark is more than an object made by ancient craftsmen—it reflects God's power in special ways. During the tribulation period when the supernatural will intersect with the natural, it is possible that the earthly ark will be found and translated to heaven—sort of an "ark rapture." I find it fitting that the ark is mentioned just seven verses after the two witnesses are translated to heaven in their personal mini-rapture.

Again, this is all speculation. In time we might learn more, but as I prayerfully write this chapter, I tend to think the ark may be found during the early part of the tribulation period and may possibly be translated to heaven's throne room along with the two witnesses at the midpoint of the tribulation.

What Goes Up Sends Something Down

As the two witnesses go up to heaven and the seventh trumpet is blown, several key events will occur. One is that Satan will be cast down from heaven. He had his citizenship revoked when he first rebelled against God, but he still has had access to the council of God in heaven (see Job 1:6-12), using whatever opportunities he can to accuse God's people. Imagine this council as a cosmic United Nations meeting where formal proceedings allow all members time to address the assembly. It is somewhat neutral ground designed for a specific purpose.

At the midpoint of the tribulation, heavenly war will commence and Satan will be cast out for good. The only problem is that he will be sent to his place of short-lived dominion—Earth. This single event will change the nature of the tribulation period in profound ways, as we will see in Revelation 12–14.

CHAPTER 10

Mega-Signs of an Epic Story

A great sign appeared in heaven: a woman clothed with the sun, with the moon under her feet and a crown of twelve stars on her head. She was pregnant and cried out in pain as she was about to give birth. Then another sign appeared in heaven: an enormous red dragon with seven heads and ten horns and seven crowns on its heads. Its tail swept a third of the stars out of the sky and flung them to the earth. The dragon stood in front of the woman who was about to give birth, so that it might devour her child the moment he was born. She gave birth to a son, a male child, who "will rule all the nations with an iron scepter." And her child was snatched up to God and to his throne.

REVELATION 12:1-5

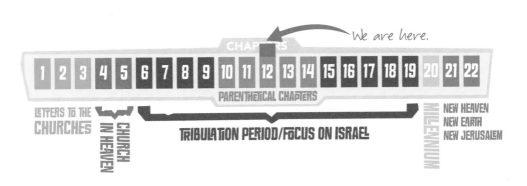

We are here.

CHAPTERS

1 2 3 4 5 6 7 8 9 10 11 12 13 14 15 16 17 18 19 20 21 22

PARENTHETICAL CHAPTERS

LETTERS TO THE CHURCHES

CHURCH IN HEAVEN

TRIBULATION PERIOD/FOCUS ON ISRAEL

MILLENNIUM

NEW HEAVEN NEW EARTH NEW JERUSALEM

There's an oft-repeated phrase in the animation industry—story is king. If the story of an animated feature film is not well developed, it doesn't matter how good the character design, animation quality, voice acting, or score are. It is human nature to love a good story. It is also human nature to intuitively sense when the story is lacking. The best animated films are the projects that spent the longest time in development. When creators and story developers do the hard work of making sure the concept truly finds its center and contains a well-developed backstory, compelling characters, and a true sense of struggle, heart, and authenticity, audiences will connect with the story.

Another key component to a compelling narrative—especially if it is episodic or contains a lot of standalone stories—is the presence of story arcs. A story arc is a theme that connects seemingly random elements in a way that moves the story forward and ties everything together in a grand scheme or meta narrative. It is an extended storyline that shows a progression and a connection. Though not seen fully in one particular event, it is the glue that holds the story together and makes it all cohesively sensible when viewed as a panoramic overlay. It is the well-crafted design of the full forest that is often overlooked when viewing a single tree.

Continuing with our film analogies, Revelation chapter 12 provides the wide establishing shot that gives us the fuller context of the key themes—the key story arcs—of Scripture and how they relate to the incredible final events of earth's history.

Communicating Through Symbols

In Revelation 1:1, we are given a great clue as to how the prophecies John wrote were conveyed to him. There we read, "The revelation from Jesus Christ, which God gave him to show his servants what must soon take place. He made it known by sending his angel to his servant John." Some translations render the phrase "made it known" as "sent and signified it." God conveyed the visions to John through signs or symbols. The Greek word used here is *esēmanen*, which essentially means to communicate through signs.

THE NON-PROPHET MISUNDERSTANDS THE USE OF SIGNS AND SYMBOLS

As mentioned previously, the book of Revelation is full of symbolism, and that symbolism can be understood either from the immediate context in which it appears or by its first mention and cross references in the Old Testament. The reason I mention the Greek term related to communicating with signs is because here in Revelation 12:1 we are told specifically that "a great sign appeared in heaven," and later in verse 3 we read that "another sign appeared." Signs point to things. They are not the actual thing. So even though Revelation can be understood literally when it describes literal events, here in Revelation 12 we are told about signs that point to a greater reality. In addition, the word "great" relating to the signs here is the Greek term *mega*. These are mega-signs. They are bigger than the moment—representing a much greater picture.

Remember that this parenthetical section of Revelation (chapters 10–14) is designed to give us the greater context for the events of Revelation. These signs described in the opening verses of Revelation 12 achieve this purpose in a sweeping fashion. In Revelation 4–9, as we studied the specific seal and trumpet judgments, we were viewing the trees, so to speak. Now the camera pulls way back to reveal the forest—the context for the book of Revelation as a whole. It speaks to a cosmic grand narrative about the battle between good and evil—between God's plan to redeem mankind and Satan's attempts to usurp God's plan and steal his throne. It's an impossible proposition, but Satan's pride has long deceived him into lusting after these goals. Revelation 12 shines a bright light on this key story arc.

Compelling Characters

Inherent to a great story are compelling, well-developed characters. These components make for a great story because they are rooted in reality. Here in the signs described in Revelation 12, we find three key characters caught up in the epic struggle between good and evil: a woman, a male child, and a great dragon. And the story goes all the way back to Satan's rebellion, the fall of mankind into sin, and the first prophecy ever given in Scripture.

QUICK FACT: DID YOU KNOW...

that Genesis 3:15 is the first prophecy in the Bible about the Messiah? It is known as the *protoevangelium*.

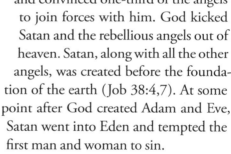

Satan was originally named Lucifer and was a beautiful guardian cherub ordained by God. You can read about his original state, rebellion, and fall in Isaiah 14:12-14 and Ezekiel 28:14-18. He was originally created sinless but with a free will. He chose to rebel against God and convinced one-third of the angels to join forces with him. God kicked Satan and the rebellious angels out of heaven. Satan, along with all the other angels, was created before the foundation of the earth (Job 38:4,7). At some point after God created Adam and Eve, Satan went into Eden and tempted the first man and woman to sin.

After the fall, God proclaimed the first prophecy as part of a curse on Satan. In Genesis 3:15, we find the first hint of a future Savior called the "offspring" or the "seed" (NASB) of the woman. By the way, this is the only place in Scripture where a woman is said to have "seed." It is the Hebrew word *zara* (zaw-rah'), applied elsewhere in Scripture only to males, or in an agricultural seed-planting context. This is an early indication that the Savior would be born of a virgin with no human male DNA. In Genesis 3:15, we read, "I will put enmity between you and the woman, and between your offspring and hers; he will crush your head, and you will strike his heel."

Notice the offspring is a *he*, and according to the prophecy he will be wounded, but in the process he will crush the head of Satan. From the moment this prophecy was given, the prideful, fallen figure known as Satan began planning how to keep the seed of the woman from fulfilling God's plan. This explains the frequent attempts through history to keep the promised male offspring from entering the scene. It explains why Cain murdered Abel, why fallen angels (somehow) produced horrific hybrid offspring with women in an attempt to corrupt the gene pool

(Genesis 6:2-4,12), Pharaoh tried to kill all Hebrew male babies, a possessed Saul constantly tried to kill David, Haman (in the book of Esther) tried to kill all Jews, Herod killed all Jewish males under two years of age, Satan tempted Jesus, and also influenced Peter to try to keep Jesus from the cross.

This story arc ties Scripture together from Genesis to Revelation in a way that brings great clarity and cohesion to the various historical accounts recorded for us in the Bible. Many people see the various stories as standalone moral lessons. But the great signs John describes in Revelation 12 remind us that all the events recorded in Scripture are intricately tied together in a great cosmic narrative. With that backdrop, let's take a look at the three characters depicted in the opening verses of Revelation 12.

The Woman

This woman with the sun, moon, and 12 stars represents Israel. If you'll recall, the drum I've been repeatedly beating is that the symbols in Revelation find their meaning in either the immediate context or the Old Testament. In Genesis

37:9-11, we read about Joseph's dream, which mentions the same symbolism of the sun, moon, and stars. Joseph was one of the 12 sons of Jacob (whose name was changed by God to Israel), and these 12 sons were the official heads of the 12 tribes of Israel. A careful study of Scripture leads us to the solid conclusion that this woman symbolizes Israel, who brought forth (i.e., gave birth to) the Messiah—Jesus.

This leads us to the next character. During the second half of the tribulation period the people of Israel will flee into the desert, where God will protect them for 1,260 days (or 3.5 years). More on this below.

The Male Child

The male child represents Jesus. Through Israel, God brought us the Scriptures and the Savior. Jesus is Jewish to the core—"the Lion of the tribe of Judah" (one of the 12 sons of Israel), the descendant of David who will one day "rule all the nations with an iron scepter" (Revelation 12:5). After Jesus completed his earthly mission, he ascended to heaven's throne.

The Dragon

The enormous red dragon represents Satan. As stated a moment ago, this evil being has attempted, at every turn, to keep the Messiah from being born—but has failed every time. His cosmic rebellion along with one-third of the angels got them all kicked out of heaven and hurled down to Earth.

I should mention that there is a mysterious twofold understanding of these great signs—as individuals and corporate entities. The woman could possibly represent both Mary individually and Israel corporately. The male child could represent Jesus individually and the church (his body) corporately, with Satan attempting to kill Jesus at birth and to destroy the church as soon as it was born (through martyrdom and persecution). The church will reign with Christ in the millennial kingdom (Revelation 20:6). The dragon could represent Satan individually and his evil beast system corporately. Satan is not omnipresent like God. He can be in only one place at a time, but his minions of fallen angels and fallen humanity make up a vast network of evil that is in place now and will reach maximum impact during the tribulation period—particularly during the second half.

A Battle in the Unseen Realm

Having already lost a cosmic boxing match at the outset of Satan's rebellion before man fell into sin, we read here about a rematch that ends the same way, except Satan is thrown further down. After the initial fall, Satan could still enter heaven's council and accuse believers before God's throne. Presently he is the prince of the power of the air, and he has a wide range of authority and freedom of movement. With this second loss to Michael (the archangel connected to key events regarding Israel throughout Scripture) and his angels, Satan completely loses his place in heaven. He and his fallen angels are cast down to Earth. Later in Revelation we'll read about two more phases of Satan's fall—to the bottomless pit during the millennial kingdom, and finally into the Lake of Fire, where he will pay for his evil ways forever.

The Danger of a Cornered Snake

After Satan's millennia-long failed attempts to keep the Savior from coming into the world in order to reconcile men and women to God, and after failing to destroy the church before it spread, Satan will shift his full focus to Plan C. If Satan can destroy all the Jewish people in the world, none of the prophecies and promises to Israel about a future kingdom on Earth (the millennial kingdom, which we'll learn about in a few chapters) would be able to be fulfilled. Satan's Plan C is an attempt to nullify God's Word and character by keeping future prophecy from being fulfilled.

A FEW PROPHECIES REQUIRING JEWISH PEOPLE IN A LITERAL FUTURE KINGDOM

ISAIAH 2:1-4 — All the nations will stream to the house of the God of Jacob.

JER. 23:5-6 — Messiah will reign as king physically, at which time Israel will be saved and dwell securely.

AMOS 9:11-12 — Jerusalem and Israel will be restored/rebuilt and will rule over the nations.

MICAH 5:2-5 — People of the Messiah will return. At that time he will rule the earth from Israel.

ZEPH. 3:14-20 — Israel will rejoice when judgments are finished. The Lord will be physically with them in Jerusalem.

In the Old Testament, Satan's fury was focused on *one* distinct group—the Jewish people. And since the first century AD, Satan has influenced world leaders, cultural forces, governments, and world events to persecute and kill *two* distinct groups of people—Jews and Christians. Because he couldn't keep the Savior from coming or the church from growing, the enemy will shift his full attention back to the destruction of the Jewish race in an attempt to keep the kingdom of the Savior from coming.

The Old Testament prophecies about the future millennial kingdom require the existence of the Jewish people, the nation of Israel, Jerusalem as the capital, and the temple in Jerusalem. Just as the "seed war" story arc (described earlier) ties together so many events in Scripture, the millennial kingdom story arc explains why the two most persecuted people groups over the past 2,000 years have been Christians and Jews.

QUICK FACT: DID YOU KNOW...

that more Christians are persecuted today than at any time in history, and antisemitism is on the rise globally?[1]

In Revelation 12:13-14, we read this:

> When the dragon saw that he had been hurled to the earth, he pursued the woman who had given birth to the male child. The woman was given the two wings of a great eagle, so that she might fly to the place prepared for her in the wilderness, where she would be taken care of for a time, times and half a time, out of the serpent's reach.

Although the enemy keeps losing, his pride never lets him give up. As Satan is thrown down to Earth at the midpoint of the tribulation, he will be filled with wrath—like a caged animal or a snake trapped in a corner—and he will turn his full attention toward attempting to destroy the Jewish race.

This is why the tribulation morphs into "the great tribulation" (Matthew 24:21 NKJV) during the second half of the seven-year period. This is also known as "the time of Jacob's [Israel's] trouble" (Jeremiah 30:7). Revelation 12:12 sheds additional light on the reasons for the increased intensity of the tribulation events and provides this warning: "Woe to the earth and the sea, because the devil has gone down to you! He is filled with fury, because he knows that his time is short."

The text further tells us that the Jewish people will flee to a place in the desert prepared for them. There, they will be protected for exactly 3.5 years. Many scholars believe the location will be ancient Petra in modern day Jordan—a rock-city fortress south of the Dead Sea. This city built into the desert mountains had been abandoned and was unknown to the world until it was rediscovered in 1812. It would make a perfect protective hiding place for a large number of people.

Revelation 12 tells us the Jewish people will escape, and that Satan will pursue them with a large army (or a literal flood of some sort), but the earth will split open and swallow up the impending danger (see verse 16). The result of this supernatural protection of the Jewish people will lead to Satan's Plan D. He failed to keep the Messiah from being born and accomplishing his mission. He failed to keep the church from spreading. He will fail to destroy the Jewish people. So Satan's Plan D—his last resort—will be to cause as much pain as possible to God by attacking "the rest of [the woman's] offspring" (Gentile tribulation believers—see the closing verse of Revelation 12).

Your Story

Did you know you are a key player in this cosmic story? If you have accepted Christ, you are mentioned in verse 10 as a brother or sister. There, the future casting down of Satan is described in these terms: "The accuser of our brothers and sisters, who accuses them before our God day and night, has been hurled down."

When we become Christians, we immediately discover that this world is not a playground, but a battleground. The enemy tempts, tries, attacks, and discourages us, and does anything he can to keep us from living effectively for our Savior. But in the end, he will fail. Verse 11 gives us the trifecta victory plan. There, we read, "They triumphed over him by the blood of the Lamb and by the word of their testimony; they did not love their lives so much as to shrink from death."

First, we triumph over the enemy by the blood of the Lamb. Jesus's sacrificial death on the cross paid our debt and won our salvation. If we receive this gift and believe in Christ for our salvation, then God views us as sinless—debt-free. The enemy's accusations no longer stick.

Second, we overcome by our testimony—that is, how we live out our faith in a fallen world. As we imperfectly strive to live for God and his purposes, we overcome the power of sin in our lives. We overcome the power of discouragement as we leverage trials and testing for God's glory. We overcome as we struggle, persevere, and long for the day of the Lord's return!

Third, we overcome in death. Even death cannot separate us from the love of God (Romans 8:38-39). You and I may not be called to serve as martyrs for our faith as most of the tribulation-period believers will be, but we are called to die daily. Galatians 5:24 says, "Those who belong to Christ Jesus have crucified the flesh with its passions and desires." Each day that we choose to die to our own sinful, selfish ways and allow God's purpose to drive us is a day that we demonstrate our deep dedication to the Lord, who sacrificed everything for us.

Though Satan is known as the "accuser of our brothers and sisters," he is an epic failure. At the moment he has a limited and short-lived jurisdiction of power and control. But as you and I overcome by the cross, our victorious lives, and our willingness to die to the ways of the world, we join the fellowship of the saints in Revelation 12:11 and can look forward to a future that gives us guaranteed victory over the enemy.

CHAPTER 11

The Unholy Fake Trinity

I wanted to know the meaning of the fourth beast, which was different from all the others and most terrifying, with its iron teeth and bronze claws—the beast that crushed and devoured its victims and trampled underfoot whatever was left.

DANIEL 7:19

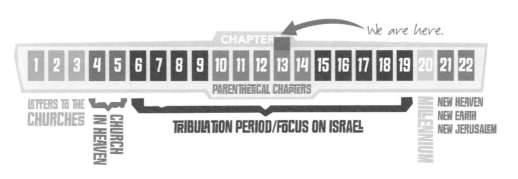

We are here.

CHAPTER

1 2 3 4 5 6 7 8 9 10 11 12 13 14 15 16 17 18 19 20 21 22

PARENTHETICAL CHAPTERS

LETTERS TO THE CHURCHES

CHURCH IN HEAVEN

TRIBULATION PERIOD/FOCUS ON ISRAEL

MILLENNIUM

NEW HEAVEN NEW EARTH NEW JERUSALEM

In one of my favorite films, *The Incredibles*, the antagonist is a villain named Syndrome. Syndrome initially idolized the protagonist, a superhero named Mr. Incredible (aka Bob Parr), and wanted to be just like him. Syndrome's real name was Buddy, and even as a boy he had great intellect and used this gift to create gadgets that mimicked real superpowers. For example, he developed rocket boots that enabled him to fly, but the boots would also malfunction at the wrong time. Mr. Incredible, on the other hand, had actual super-powers—namely, extraordinary strength and toughness. He could stop trains, killer robots, and anything else that came his way, and even after intense battles he would barely have a scratch on him.

Years after their initial encounters, Buddy grew up and became Syndrome—a villainous figure who used his gift of invention for evil purposes. He wanted to be like Mr. Incredible, but he didn't have the innate powers. His pride and bitterness led him to work against superheroes by creating counterfeit superhero technology. He had a strategic mind, faux superpowers, and an evil heart—a dangerous combination. After several apparent victories throughout the movie, his evil pride eventually led to his complete destruction.

We find a similar jealousy in Satan. He has always wanted to be like God, but he doesn't have what it takes. There is only one true God, and he has no equal. Scripture is clear on that. Satan is not omnipresent, omniscient, omnipotent. Ultimately, he is doomed to failure, and we know his final outcome. We've read the back of the book. He will be soundly defeated and punished. We as believers, on the other hand, will be victorious because of what Jesus accomplished on the cross 2,000 years ago.

SATAN		GOD
CREATED	AGE	ETERNAL
ONE PLACE AT A TIME	PRESENCE	OMNIPRESENT (EVERYWHERE AT ONCE)
FINITE/LIMITED	POWER	OMNIPOTENT (ALL-POWERFUL)
FINITE/LIMITED	KNOWLEDGE	OMNISCIENT (ALL-KNOWING)
EVIL	NATURE	HOLY/PERFECT
DEFEATED	RECORD	UNDEFEATED

In the meantime—and especially during the tribulation period—the enemy will mimic God in his own twisted way. Satan can't create anything new. He merely counterfeits what God does, using things God has already created. Many assume Satan wants to produce atheists, but he doesn't. He wants worshipers. During the tribulation, Satan will finally have his man of the hour—the antichrist, an evil world dictator and a fake messiah. We learn in 2 Thessalonians 2:3-4 that this individual will not be revealed until after the rapture. This future world ruler will be supported by another evil figure known as the false prophet. Together, Satan, the antichrist, and the false prophet will form a twisted, counterfeit trinity of sorts. We are given a detailed description of the antichrist and the false prophet here in Revelation 13.

The Sea Beast

Revelation 13:1-3—I saw a beast coming out of the sea. It had ten horns and seven heads, with ten crowns on its horns, and on each head a blasphemous name. The beast I saw resembled a leopard, but had feet like those of a bear and a mouth like that of a lion. The dragon gave the beast his power and his throne and great authority. One of the heads of the beast seemed to have had a fatal wound, but the fatal wound had been healed. The whole world was filled with wonder and followed the beast.

The sea is often a metaphor in Scripture for chaos or turbulence. It is also used to reference the populace (as in a "sea of people"), and specifically people from a distant area (Psalm 144:7; Isaiah 17:12; 60:5; Ezekiel 26:3). This first beast is none other than the antichrist, who will arise out of a large population of directionless people at the most turbulent time in history.

Based on Daniel 9:26-27, it seems the antichrist will most likely come from somewhere in Western Europe. He will come from the same region as that of the people who destroyed Jerusalem in AD 70 ("the people of the ruler who will come"). Jerusalem and the temple were destroyed by the armies of the Roman commander (and later emperor) Titus, who was born in Rome and served in both Britain and Germany before commanding the legion in Judea beginning in AD 67.[1]

The antichrist will likely be a progressive, globalist elite from Western Europe. Not all prophecy experts agree on this, but I believe this view has the best scriptural support. Some believe he could rise out of America (colonized out of an area of ancient Rome and containing a Roman form of government, architecture, and similar growing moral implosion), while others posit that the antichrist will come from a Muslim nation (arising from the Eastern leg of what was formerly the Roman Empire, which split from the Western leg in AD 285).

As the state of the world grows increasingly precarious with each passing day, we seem to be more and more on the verge of financial and geopolitical collapse. Eventually there will come a major global event that pushes us over the edge. In fact, the rapture of the church will instantly plunge the world into the most chaotic time in all of history, and the light-bearing, sin-restraining influence of the church will be gone. One expert likens the rapture to God turning the lights out on Earth. Everything will descend immediately into chaos and spiritual darkness.

Out of this turbulence will rise a smooth-talking globalist with a convincing master plan to bring order out of chaos. Unfortunately for the people of the world, it will be a lie—a great deception. The beast from the sea depicted in Revelation 13 is none other than the antichrist. We know from Daniel 7:24 and Revelation 17:12 that the ten horns represent ten elite end-time rulers who will reign with the antichrist until he subdues three of them. Then there will be seven. So there will be seven rulers over ten nations or geographic areas. Then, as we saw in our study of Revelation 6 and the seal judgments, the antichrist will be given global authority and great military might.

When Daniel explained the meaning of the statue that appeared in Nebuchadnezzar's dream (Daniel 2), he described the four world empires as different kinds of metals. In this way, the kingdoms are viewed from man's perspective. Later, in Daniel 7, we see the same empires from God's perspective, and they are beasts. First Samuel 16:7 tells us, "People look at the outward appearance, but the LORD looks at the heart." This principle applies in Daniel 7 as God describes the four empires as looking like a lion, a bear, a leopard, and a hideous beast—the same symbolism we see here in Revelation 13.

The world will embrace the antichrist as a savior, but God will see him for what he truly is—a savage beast. And this beast will mimic his master—Satan. Scripture tells us that the devil "masquerades as an angel of light" (2 Corinthians 11:14), but from God's perspective, he is a roaring lion seeking to devour people (1 Peter 5:8) as well as a slithering serpent (Genesis 3).

The antichrist will receive some type of a fatal—or seemingly so—wound that will be miraculously healed (Revelation 13:3). This counterfeit resurrection will mimic that of Christ's and will garner the wonder and worship of many. Satan always copies and twists what God does. Here, with John's account of the beast of the sea, we find a false messiah, an antichrist. *Anti* means "against," but it can also mean "in place of." In 1 John 2:18, we learn that many antichrists (false saviors) have and will come during the church age, but there will be one specific end-time antichrist according to Revelation 13, several chapters of Daniel, 2 Thessalonians 2:3-4, and other passages in Scripture.

WHO IS THE ANTICHRIST?

"the little horn"	**Daniel 7:8**
"a fierce-looking king"	**Daniel 8:23**
"a master of intrigue"	**Daniel 8:23**
"the ruler who will come"	**Daniel 9:26**
"a contemptible person"	**Daniel 11:21**
"a shepherd who will not care"	**Zechariah 11:16**
"a worthless shepherd"	**Zechariah 11:16-17**
"man of lawlessness"	**2 Thessalonians 2:3**
"the lawless one"	**2 Thessalonians 2:8-9**
"the rider on the white horse"	**Revelation 6:2**
"a beast"	**Revelation 13:1**

The Enemy's End-Game

> *Revelation 13:4-8*—People worshiped the dragon because he had given authority to the beast, and they also worshiped the beast and asked, "Who is like the beast? Who can wage war against it?" The beast was given a mouth to utter proud words and blasphemies and to exercise its authority for forty-two months. It opened its mouth to blaspheme God, and to slander his name and his dwelling place and those who live in heaven. It was given power to wage war against God's holy people and to conquer them. And it was given authority over every tribe, people, language and nation. All inhabitants of the earth will worship the beast—all whose names have not been written in the Lamb's book of life, the Lamb who was slain from the creation of the world.

The result of the antichrist's deadly wound being healed will be worship—of Satan and the antichrist. The world will clearly see that the authority and power of the antichrist comes from Satan, who is portrayed here (as in Revelation 12) as a dragon. In the Gospel accounts of the temptation of Jesus in the desert, we read that Satan offered Jesus the kingdoms of the world (Matthew 4:8-10). We are given every indication that the offer was real. Satan hoped Jesus would accept and agree to worship him. Jesus refused, but the end-time ruler known as the antichrist will readily accept Satan's offer.

According to Revelation 13:4, people will ask, "Who is like the beast?" This question is yet another satanic counterfeit of something God had already established. For example, the psalmist asked in Psalm 113:5, "Who is like the LORD our God, the One who sits enthroned on high?" Satan has always wanted worship. He will receive it openly by the masses during the tribulation. Satan, because of his hatred for God, will empower the antichrist to "utter proud words and blasphemies" (Revelation 13:5). The antichrist will have a global platform, and for 3.5 years (42 months) he will slander God's name, throne, and children. Though he will show up as a peacemaker at the opening of the first seal at the beginning of the tribulation period, he will wage all-out global war on believers by the midpoint.

The Earth Beast

Revelation 13:11-13—I saw a second beast, coming out of the earth. It had two horns like a lamb, but it spoke like a dragon. It exercised all the authority of the first beast on its behalf and made the earth and its inhabitants worship the first beast, whose fatal wound had been healed. And it performed great signs, even causing fire to come down from heaven to the earth in full view of the people.

Here in Revelation 13 we are also introduced to a second beast. Whereas the first beast came out of the sea, this one will come out of the earth. Much like the demonic locusts of the abyss, the lying power and deceptive intent of this figure will come straight from the pit of hell. Though depicted as a religious leader (a lamb), this beast will speak like a dragon (a symbol of Satan). This figure is known as the false prophet. He will be a religious leader who unifies the world in worship of the beast. He will have satanically empowered abilities that will blow people's minds. The purpose of his supernatural powers will be to deceive the world. Together, Satan, the antichrist, and the false prophet will form an unholy trinity of sorts—a twisted counterfeit of the real Triune Godhead of the Father, Son, and Holy Spirit.

The Beast System

Revelation 13:14-18—Because of the signs it was given power to perform on behalf of the first beast, it deceived the inhabitants of the earth. It ordered them to set up an image in honor of the beast who was wounded by the sword and yet lived. The second beast was given power to give breath to the image of the first beast, so that the image could speak and cause all who refused to worship the image to be killed. It also forced all people, great and small, rich and poor, free and slave, to receive a mark on their right hands or on their foreheads, so that they could not buy or sell unless they had the mark, which is the name of the beast or the number of its name. This calls for wisdom. Let the person who has insight calculate the number of the beast, for it is the number of a man. That number is 666.

The end-time global government supported by a satanically deceptive world-wide religion will result in an all-inclusive system of oppression and destruction led by the most depraved ruler the world has ever known. In Revelation 13:14-18, we learn that the false prophet will leverage his power and influence to propagate this malevolent beast system. The false prophet will, in some way, bring an idol of the antichrist to life. This image of the beast will have the ability to kill any who refuse to worship the antichrist idol. The false prophet will also institute a global cashless system that will require everyone on earth to receive a mark (possibly an implant or digital tattoo) in order to purchase daily necessities or conduct business of any kind.

The mark these tribulation-era people will receive will be linked to antichrist, contain some form of end-time technology, and relate in some fashion to the number 666. Scripturally speaking, six is the number of man (man was created on the sixth day), and the antichrist will be "man cubed" or man to the fullest extent Satan can take him. Humanism is the driving secular philosophy of the day and it will be played out in full during the tribulation. This number could also possibly relate to *gematria*, which is a method of assigning numbers to letters in various alphabets in languages such as Arabic, Greek, or Hebrew.

There is so much here that I'd love to unpack related to the technology that is in place now or emerging in our day that is very likely to be a part of the beast's future economic network. God could accomplish everything described in this chapter via supernatural means, but it seems that God's timing works in such a way that his ordained events coincide with real-time technological and geo-political developments. For example, the extensive Roman road system, the widespread use of the Greek language, and the conditions established by Pax Romana (a period of peace in the Roman Empire from 27 BC to AD 180) all made for the perfect conditions for Christ's first coming and the spread of the gospel.

> Galatians 4:4 —When the set time had fully come, God sent his Son.

In my previous book, *The Non-Prophet's Guide™ to the End Times*, I wrote an entire chapter on the signs of technology. In one section I discuss the beast's economic network at length, pointing out how all the technology needed for such a system already exists today. Cashless systems, giant data storage facilities, artificial intelligence, super-processing capabilities, and several viable candidates for mark technology are all well developed and in widespread use today. More than ever, the world is connected, surveilled, and prepared for mark technology, and these technologies are all about to experience exponential growth.

Some prophecy experts also highlight the possibility that the mark of the beast may also be used to change people in some significant biological way. Revelation tells us that once someone takes the mark of the beast, he or she will have arrived at the point of no return and can no longer be saved (Revelation 14:10-11). We also find that only those who take the mark of the beast will later have painful sores all over their bodies (Revelation 16:2). This could mean that something biological—such as faulty DNA editing or other emerging technology—about the mark will cause these sores.

Artificial Intelligence (AI) and the Image of the Beast

Worshiping a carved image may seem too archaic to our modern sensibilities, but an artificial intelligence-based idol that could come alive, speak, think, and kill may very well be the technology Satan uses as part of the beast system. As mentioned earlier in this book, emerging autonomous weapons—including drones, miniature drone swarms, killer robots, and the like—are already many years into development by various militaries around the world.

THE NON-PROPHET ON AI

AI CONSISTENTLY BEATS THE WORLD'S BEST HUMAN CHESS PLAYERS AND WILL DRIVE AUTONOMOUS CARS.

RRIIIIGHT.

TALK ABOUT ARTIFICIAL INTELLIGENCE.

It seems from Revelation 13:14-18 that the image of the beast may be technologically integrated with mark-of-the-beast capabilities and connected to some type of satanically driven AI that will give the image life. It is not clear from the passage whether the image is a specific idol in one location, or if each worshiping household or person will have an idol of the beast. In either case, the ancient demonic practice of idol worship will be prevalent again during the tribulation period, but likely with some new techno-logical and demonic twists that will make it even more diabolical.

Spotting Counterfeits

The best way to spot a counterfeit is to be familiar with the real thing. People who are trained to spot counterfeit money don't spend much time studying fake money. They spend their time studying the real cash. They become so familiar with the real thing that counterfeits become easy to spot.

I'm sad to say that although we have more Bibles, Bible study tools, churches, archeological and textual support for the reli-ability of Scripture, and a clearer understanding of fulfilled prophecy than any other time in history, every recent study shows that Christians are less biblically literate than ever. The less God's people know God's Word, the less equipped they are to spot error and decep-tion by the enemy.

What can we do in response? You and I can first make a personal commitment to studying the entire Bible. There are many plans available that can help you read through the Bible in a year. Doing this takes about 15-20 minutes a day. Second, we can study Bible prophecy, which touches on every aspect of theology and provides great clarity and confidence for everyday living—especially as we see how God backs up his promises by fulfilling prophecies exactly as foretold.

In 2 Timothy 2:15, we read this: "Do your best to present yourself to God as one approved, a worker who does not need to be ashamed and who correctly han-dles the word of truth." Simply attending church one day a week is not going to cut it. We need God's Word like we need oxygen, food, or water. I know I'm sounding a little preachy here, but we are dropping the ball as believers if we are not immersing ourselves daily in Scripture, and we need to equip our-selves to help people who are falling for deception as we inch ever closer to the time of the end.

Jesus himself warned in Matthew 24:24, "False messiahs and false prophets will appear and perform great signs and wonders to deceive, if possible, even the elect." Did you catch that? The deception leading up to, and during, the tribulation period will be so diabolically convincing that—*if* possible—it has the potential to deceive even true believers. That is, these signs and wonders *shouldn't* fool us, but if we don't know the core fundamentals of Christianity and the basics of biblical teaching, we leave ourselves susceptible to deception.

As the stage-setting continues and the message of the gospel becomes less and less popular, let's focus our attention on studying God's Word, worshiping him, and prayerfully sharing the love and message of Christ with the world. One of the great deceptions of today that will become more widespread during the early part of the tribulation is that Jesus is merely *a* way to God. One way among many. As this watered-down teaching creeps into Christendom, hold true to God's Word. Jesus is still *the* way, *the* truth, and *the* life (John 14:6). Anything else is a counterfeit.

CHAPTER 12

Three Earth-Circling Angels and Seven Angry Bowls

I looked, and there before me was the Lamb, standing on Mount Zion, and with him 144,000 who had his name and his Father's name written on their foreheads.

REVELATION 14:1

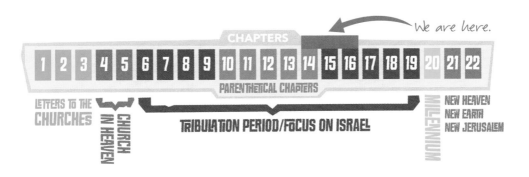

We are here.

CHAPTERS

1 2 3 4 5 6 7 8 9 10 11 12 13 14 15 16 17 18 19 20 21 22

PARENTHETICAL CHAPTERS

LETTERS TO THE CHURCHES — CHURCH IN HEAVEN — TRIBULATION PERIOD/FOCUS ON ISRAEL — MILLENNIUM — NEW HEAVEN NEW EARTH NEW JERUSALEM

Over the years I've worked on several long-term creative projects (including this book), and there's one experience that I've encountered almost every time. After many months of hard work I will assess where the project stands, only to realize I'm just halfway finished. While all of these projects have been a labor of love, they have also been hard work. I call this experience the *messy middle*.

You know you've reached the messy middle when you feel like you've given just about everything to the task at hand, but you still have a long way to go. You then wonder if you have what it takes to finish. Runners call this *hitting the wall*. This phenomenon is true whether it comes to writing books, persevering through long struggles, enduring intense workouts or sports competitions, and anything else that takes effort, determination, and stamina. Without some type of motivating force it is difficult to press on, and oftentimes you simply have to

grind it out. As you focus your attention on what to do next and put one foot in front of the other, before you know it, you'll have moved the ball forward a few yards, and eventually you'll cross the goal line.

That's what's been happening so far as we make our way through Revelation. A lot has been happening and we're just approaching the midpoint. But here in chapter 14, we get to take a short breather. We're given an encouraging vision of the end of the tribulation. When dark times hit and there seems to be no end in sight, capturing a glimpse of the future payoff can mean the difference between giving up in despair or pressing on toward that future hope.

Revelation 14 serves as a transitional link between the mid-trib events detailed in chapters 10–13 and the events of the second half of the tribulation detailed in Revelation 15–16. For that reason, I have provided an overview of all three chapters below. These chapters begin with an amazing glimpse of a promised future—exactly the respite needed before returning to the horrific judgments that will come forth during second half of the tribulation.

Flash Forward

The opening verses of Revelation 14 provide a flash-forward glimpse of a climactic event at the end of the tribulation period, just before the arrival of the millennial kingdom. In Revelation 7 we were introduced to the 144,000 Jewish evangelists—whose ministry will lead to the salvation of many during the tribulation. Here in chapter 14, we bump into them again as we read about a zenith moment predicted by the Old Testament prophets. John describes the scene at the end of the tribulation, when the Messiah will come and stand on Mount Zion with the 144,000 whom he has preserved through the seven years of tribulation. The Jewish people have longed for this event to take place, and still do.

Jewish followers of Christ understand that this event is related to the second coming of Jesus, but traditional Judaism teaches that the first arrival of the Messiah on Mount Zion has yet to happen. To Jews who are not yet Christians, the church age is still a mystery. Paul tells us these individuals are partially blind to the truth and won't understand this until the fullness of the Gentiles have been saved (see Romans 9–11). I say partially because throughout church history there has been a remnant of Jewish people who have recognized that Jesus was the promised Messiah.

It's important to note that Revelation details three distinct groups of Jewish people: the 144,000 evangelists whose ministry will start around the beginning of the tribulation period, a large number of unbelieving Jewish people who will embrace the antichrist and his treaty, and a small remnant who will accept Christ as their Messiah—some of whom will survive to the end of the tribulation by hiding in a place prepared for them in advance.

As we learned in Revelation 12, a remnant of the Jewish people will be kept safe in a place "prepared" in advance for them (verse 14). For several reasons derived from clues in Scripture, most prophecy scholars believe this will be the ancient fortified city of Petra. If it weren't for God's protection and provision, all Jewish people would be killed by the Hitler-dwarfing campaign of the future antichrist.

Scripture tells us that one-third of the world's Jewish people will survive the tribulation period. This includes the 144,000 Jewish evangelists. The remnant that accepts Christ will join Gentile believers to reign with Christ during the 1,000-year millennial kingdom. More on that later.

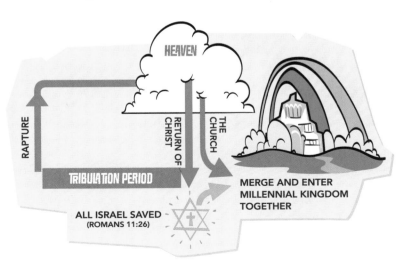

HEAVEN

RAPTURE

RETURN OF CHRIST

THE CHURCH

TRIBULATION PERIOD

ALL ISRAEL SAVED (ROMANS 11:26)

MERGE AND ENTER MILLENNIAL KINGDOM TOGETHER

The Jewish people have been through so much persecution throughout their history. It is truly heartbreaking to know the worst is yet to come. As difficult as it is to swallow this bad news, I would rather hear a hard truth than a soft lie. God shoots straight. He doesn't mince words or cater to our fallen sensibilities.

It is encouraging to know that Paul's words in Romans 11:25-27 will be fulfilled at the end of the tribulation period. There, he says that "all Israel will be saved." Revelation 14:1 depicts the glorious moment when the 144,000 sealed and protected Jewish evangelists will stand with their promise-keeping Messiah in Jerusalem!

John describes Jesus himself (the Lamb) standing on Mount Zion with the 144,000. This is the very place where Abraham's faith was tested when he was told to offer his son Isaac as a sacrifice. It's also the same spot that later became the site of Solomon's Temple. Mount Zion includes the surrounding area of Jerusalem, where Jesus was crucified immediately outside the city walls. This small area of land is truly the epicenter of God's activity throughout history.

QUICK FACT: DID YOU KNOW...

that *Zion* appears in the Old Testament 152 times as a title of Jerusalem?[1]

By the way, many Bible students (myself included) believe that the Angel of the Lord who halted Abraham's sacrifice of Isaac is none other than the preincarnate Jesus! God provided a lamb and Isaac was spared, but at the time of Abraham's faith test, it would be another 2,000 years before the Lamb was sacrificed on the cross.

John 1:29—The next day John saw Jesus coming toward him and said, "Look, the Lamb of God, who takes away the sin of the world!"

Three Earth-Circling Angels

Next we encounter three angels who will make pronouncements to "every nation, tribe, language and people" (14:6,8,9). These include proclaiming the "eternal gospel," a declaration that Babylon the Great has fallen, a warning to people not to worship the beast or his image, and a warning not to receive his mark on their forehead or hand.

Once again, God's merciful character is shown. Even though the world will reject the preaching of the two witnesses and the 144,000, he will send an angel to preach the gospel to everyone. Jewish prophecy is often circular or cyclical. We know from Matthew 24 that the gospel will go out to every area of the world before the rapture. Then here in Revelation 14 we read that once again the gospel will go out to the whole world before the return of Christ.

The next angel will preach doom. God always offers grace before judgment falls. He is a just God who must punish sin, but he always offers grace first. Babylon and its evil system will collapse. The defeat and judgment of evil is as good as done. It is a sure thing, and the second angel will boldly proclaim the sure destruction of the antichrist's evil system once and for all.

The third angel will clear up any ambiguity and gives the world some practical advice that will be immediately relevant to its hearers. In no uncertain terms, this angel will let people know that those who choose to side with the antichrist (and with Satan by default)—via taking the mark and worshiping the beast and his image—will be punished "for ever and ever." The angel will further proclaim that "there will be no rest day or night for those who worship the beast and its image, or for anyone who receives the mark of its name" (verse 11).

Satan is not the CEO of hell, and hell is not a place where those who live like the devil will get to go and party together. It will be a place of unfathomable loneliness, destruction, regret, and torment. A partial definition of hell is the absolute absence of God and his blessings. And the third angel's job will be to give a final warning. This will not be a test of the emergency God-cast system. It will be the real deal—the final opportunity for people worldwide to pick sides, and as a result, seal their destiny.

Harvest and Winepress

Again, we're taken on a flash-forward journey to the end of the tribulation. On the heels of the third angel's sobering message comes the harvest. Gentle Jesus, meek and mild, is now depicted with a sharp sickle in his hand—the ultimate grim reaper. Playtime is over. Grace has run dry and the cup of God's wrath is full and about to tip over and pour out upon the earth in full strength.

More angels are introduced at the end of Revelation 14. The first one "swung his sickle over the earth, and the earth was harvested" (verse 16). Another angel is told to "gather the clusters of grapes" (verse 18), and he threw them into the "great winepress of God's wrath" (verse 19). Verse 20 describes the gruesome results of the final battle (which we'll discuss more later) in the valley below Jerusalem, where blood will flow "as high as the horses' bridles." The armies of the world who side with the antichrist will find their fate in the worst bloodbath in the history of mankind. That's a scene you'll never see on a coffee mug.

I often hear people say, in essence, "The God of the Old Testament was a God of wrath and violence, but I worship the God of the New Testament, who is full of grace and love." I want to say to them, "Um, have you ever read Revelation? Check out Revelation 14:14-20 and get back to me." God is love, as

Scripture tells us, but love must punish evil. Jesus paid our sin debt in full. That is love. This is also the only way we can be made right with God.

In John 14:6, Jesus said, "I am the way and the truth and the life. No one comes to the Father except through me." That is as clear as it gets. Acts 4:12 plainly teaches, "Salvation is found in no one else, for there is no other name under heaven given to mankind by which we must be saved." We're also told in no uncertain terms in 2 Peter 3:9 that God does not want anyone to perish. Why else would he have sent his Son to die for mankind?

God has done everything possible for people to escape judgment, but a time is coming when the last call will be over and God's judgment must arrive. This flash-forward to the end of the tribulation depicts that moment in unadulterated detail.

Seven Bowl Judgments Set Up (Revelation 15)

I boxed for a few years as a teenager, and I still train, spar, and do an occasional match. Some boxers have what's known as natural cardio. I am not one of those boxers. No matter how hard I train, my cardio is always my toughest opponent. In between rounds, my main goal is always to get oxygen back into my lungs, and the last thing I do before the next round begins is take a big, deep breath of air.

This shortest chapter in Revelation is like a pause between rounds, and it is a final moment of calm before the extreme judgments that will mop things up on earth and bring in everlasting righteousness. Revelation 15 is like taking a deep breath before stepping back into the ring for the final round.

With the flash-forward description fresh on our minds, at the opening of chapter 15 John sees another "great and marvelous sign." He sees seven more angels with the "seven last plagues—last, because with them God's wrath is completed" (15:1). Along with the seven angels John catches another glimpse of heaven's throne room. This is a prelude to the last seven judgments to be poured out by God, which are known as the bowl judgments.

Seven Bowl Descriptions (Revelation 16)

A few years ago, I had the flu. Not a cold, not a bug, but the full-blown flu. Fever, aches, headache, cough, congestion—the whole enchilada. My dad has said,

"You know you have the flu when you feel like you're going to die but you don't." True words! I hadn't experienced the flu since I was about ten years old. When you are a child, you have no frame of reference and simply endure what the flu brings, and you seem to bounce back quicker. Or, maybe you just tend to forget the pain and discomfort after the ordeal is over.

Anyway, I must have forgotten how bad the flu was. About three days into my sickness at around 9:00 p.m., I remember saying to myself, "Okay, this must be the worst of it because I don't see how I can get any worse." Then I woke up at 3:00 a.m. and I felt much, much worse! I learned that there are levels of hardship, and there is always something worse.

The three sets of judgments described in Revelation get progressively worse. Here in Revelation 16, they are as bad as they can get. In previous judgments we saw God holding himself back. For example, he would allow only one-third of the world's trees to be destroyed, or one-third of the sun to be darkened. But here, when it comes time for the final bowl judgments, there's no holding back. No pulling punches. To use another boxing analogy: Every swing has bad intentions.

The first bowl judgment will result in "ugly, festering sores" on those who accept the mark of the beast (verse 2). As I mentioned in an earlier chapter, this may have to do with DNA manipulation gone bad, some kind of nuclear poisoning, or perhaps the breakdown of RFID chips implanted with the mark. Scripture doesn't tell us the cause of the sores, but it seems logical that they will somehow be related to the mark.

The second bowl judgment will turn the entire ocean into blood, killing everything in it. Can you imagine the worldwide stench?! I don't know whether this refers to literal blood, or to what is known today as "red tide," where tiny microorganisms multiply rapidly and turn sea water red and deplete it of oxygen—resulting in massive deaths of sea life. It is interesting to note that incidents of red tide have been on the rise in recent years.

The third bowl judgment will have the same effect on the earth's rivers and springs, causing every major water source on earth to become polluted. This judgment is reminiscent of one of the judgments Moses leveled on ancient Egypt.

The fourth bowl judgment seems to include a massive breakdown of the earth's atmosphere or massive solar flares or coronal mass ejections. People will be scorched by the sun and "seared by the intense heat" (verse 9). Yet we are told they will still refuse to repent and glorify God.

The fifth bowl judgment will plunge the beast's kingdom into darkness. Again, this is similar to a judgment Moses brought upon ancient Egypt when Pharaoh refused to let the Israelites go. Even so, people will take their rebellion a step further and curse God.

The sixth bowl judgment will dry up the Euphrates River to "prepare the way for the kings from the East" (verse 12). These will be massive armies from Asia that travel to join the final end-time battle described below.

Before the seventh bowl judgment is described, John gives a horrific glimpse of the utter darkness and evil of the counterfeit trinity. Out of the mouths of the dragon, the beast, and the false prophet will come demonic frog-like spirits for the express purpose of churning the rebellion of the world's rulers into a hate-filled frenzy bent on warring against God.

Think about that for a moment: Human beings will attempt to take on God. At this point, perhaps they even know that Christ's return is imminent. They have heard the preaching of the 144,000, the 2 witnesses, and the 3 angels. Up to this point, all their rebellious plans will have failed. All that is left for them to do, as a last resort, is to pool their resources and hatred and declare physical war on the coming Messiah. How foolish.

John tells us that the armies of the earth will gather at the Mount of Megiddo (aka Armageddon), a vast plain north of Jerusalem that has been the scene of many battles over the past few thousand years. Alexander the Great is said to have proclaimed this was the best place he had ever seen to stage an army for battle. Many people refer to this conflict as the battle of Armageddon, but more accurately, there will be several stages to this end-time war. It will begin on the plains of Megiddo before moving through Israel, down into southern Jordan, then back up to Jerusalem. More correctly, this conflict should be called the campaign of Armageddon.

CAMPAIGN OF
ARMAGEDDON

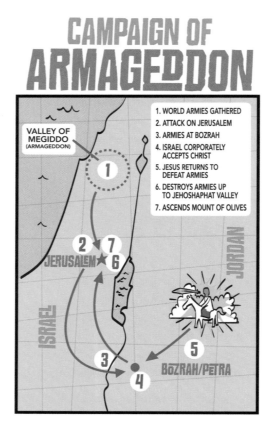

1. WORLD ARMIES GATHERED
2. ATTACK ON JERUSALEM
3. ARMIES AT BOZRAH
4. ISRAEL CORPORATELY ACCEPTS CHRIST
5. JESUS RETURNS TO DEFEAT ARMIES
6. DESTROYS ARMIES UP TO JEHOSHAPHAT VALLEY
7. ASCENDS MOUNT OF OLIVES

VALLEY OF MEGIDDO (ARMAGEDDON)

JERUSALEM

ISRAEL

JORDAN

BoZRAH/PETRA

The seventh bowl judgment will include the worst earthquake the world has ever seen. The earthquake related to the sixth seal judgment that occurs during the first half of the tribulation will move mountains and islands from their places, indicating a possible pole or crustal shift. The tribulation era's final major earthquake, by contrast, will cause entire cities to collapse, Jerusalem to split into three parts, every island to sink, and every mountain to crumble. If that weren't bad enough, 100-pound hailstones will fall on the armies assembled to fight God. These idolaters will receive an old-fashioned cosmic stoning at the hands of almighty God.

Rewind

In the final throes of the judgment upon the earth, God will take the globe like a ball of Play-Doh and squish it all together to prepare it for what will become a recreated earth for the millennial kingdom. He will wipe the slate clean and start fresh, returning the earth to its initial form before sin entered the scene. But before we get into the millennial kingdom, which is described for us in Revelation 20, or the eternal state in Revelation 21–22, we must first look at the fall of the evil world religious and political systems—as portrayed in Revelation 17–19.

CHAPTER 13

The End of Babylon's Babbling

On her forehead a name was written:

MYSTERY, BABYLON THE GREAT,
THE MOTHER OF HARLOTS
AND OF THE ABOMINATIONS
OF THE EARTH.

REVELATION 17:5 (NKJV)

We are here.

CHAPTERS

1 2 3 4 5 6 7 8 9 10 11 12 13 14 15 16 17 18 19 20 21 22

PARENTHETICAL CHAPTERS

LETTERS TO THE CHURCHES

CHURCH IN HEAVEN

TRIBULATION PERIOD/FOCUS ON ISRAEL

MILLENNIUM

NEW HEAVEN
NEW EARTH
NEW JERUSALEM

If you want to trace good and evil in the Bible, just follow the history of Jerusalem and Babylon. Jerusalem is called the city of God. Babylon, on the other hand, had a rebellious and evil beginning and this theme carries through all of Scripture—culminating here in Revelation 17 and 18, where we read about the city's future destruction. Babylon is both a place and a system, similar to how we refer to Wall Street, which is both a literal location and a financial entity.

BEHOLD—THE ORIGIN OF BABYLON'S NAME!

WHEN GOD CONFUSED THE LANGUAGES, NO ONE COULD UNDERSTAND EACH OTHER, SO GOD SAID, "BABBLE ON. BABBLE ON."

OLD TESTAMENT LINGUISTICS

A Tale of Two Babylons

Babylon shows up in two key forms in the Old Testament. First, in a man-centered, God-defying religious form as described in the account of Nimrod and the Tower of Babel (Genesis 11). Second, around 1,650 years later we read about Babylon again, this time in a wealthy and conquering political form under Nebuchadnezzar.

Chapters 17–18 of Revelation detail the future destruction of both a religious Babylon (called Mystery Babylon) and a political/economic Babylon (called Babylon the Great). The context (two collapses, two announcing angels, two systems, detailed in two separate chapters) lets us know that these are describing two events or possibly two cities representing different entities (religious and political) within the overall Babylonian system—one being led by the false prophet and the other by the antichrist.

The Rise and Fall of the False Prophet

In Revelation 17, John is "carried…away in the spirit" to see a vision—a woman riding a beast. She is referred to as the great prostitute. In verse 5, we read that she has these titles written on her forehead: "Babylon the Great" and "The Mother of All Prostitutes and of the Abominations of the Earth." The first speaks to its power, the second to its broad and evil influence.

QUICK FACT: DID YOU KNOW...

that the European Union often uses the symbolism of a woman (the goddess Europa) riding a beast?

John said he was astonished until the angel explained what he was seeing. The beast is the antichrist described in a previous chapter, but also the global corporate beast system. In Revelation 13:1, we saw that he had seven heads and ten crowns, and we see the same here. We also saw earlier that he had been given a fatal wound, which was followed by a resurrection of sorts. We find similar language here about the beast who "once was, now is not, and will come up out of the Abyss and go to its destruction" (Revelation 17:8).

John informs us that once the antichrist is done consolidating his power and he no longer needs the false prophet, he will "hate" him and destroy him and his system of religious influence and control (verse 16). This is, in fact, how dictators of the fairly recent past have operated as well. It was true with Hitler's Germany, and it was true with Soviet Communism. People are religious by nature, and evil rulers leverage this fact to consolidate power and take control. This probably means that the religious Babylon system will be destroyed by the antichrist. Later in Revelation we find the antichrist and the false prophet both judged and thrown "alive" into the Lake of Fire, which seems to indicate it's not the false prophet who is destroyed, but the religious system. If the false prophet were to be killed, then he would have to be resurrected in order to face God's judgment.

We know from Revelation 13 that the false prophet will help the antichrist set up his image and will demand that the citizens of the world take the mark of the beast or die. Apparently, after this is accomplished, the antichrist will then turn against the false prophet and destroy his religious system.

Ancient Babylon

The first appearance of Babylon in Scripture is in the account detailed in Genesis 11. There, we read about how Nimrod—a descendant of Noah—developed an anti-God religion and leveraged his influence to build a city with a tower that was designed to reach heaven. This may have been an attempt to protect against another future deluge judgment—in unbelief of God's promise that he would never again judge the world by flood. There was a lot more going on here than just a rebellious man with aspirations to build a skyscraper tall enough to pierce heaven's zip code. This was an attempt to build a global political and religious system in rebellion against God. It was a satanically led merging of technology, human-centered occult religion, and global government.

QUICK FACT: DID YOU KNOW...
the European Union also identifies with the Tower of Babel, and the EU HQ building in Brussels resembles the Tower of Babel from Peter Bruegel's famous painting?

On a much smaller scale, there is a sense in which that's what people are trying to do today when they use an Ouija board or consult with a medium. *Babylon* means "gateway to god" or "the gateway to the gods." Several times in Scripture, fallen angels are referred to as lowercase-*g* gods. At the tower of Babel, man and evil entities were attempting to work together through the veil that separates the seen and unseen realms in open defiance against the Lord.

History informs us that Nimrod had a wife named Semiramis. Before marriage, she had a son named Tammuz, whom she claimed was supernaturally placed in her womb, thus making him a savior child born of a virgin.

Ancient stories about Tammuz say he was gored by a boar, died, was dead for 40 days, then came back to life. Sound familiar? Again, Satan is always the master (but twisted) counterfeiter. Based on the prophecy in Genesis 3:15 of a future virgin-born Savior, Satan was attempting to place his chess piece on the board with early plans to deceive the world. Semiramis and Tammuz came to be worshiped, and Semiramis came to be known as "the Queen of Heaven."

As history marched forward, the same basic counterfeit-gospel story (virgin mother, savior baby killed and resurrected), and immoral occult practices have proliferated in various key empires around the world. Only the names have changed.

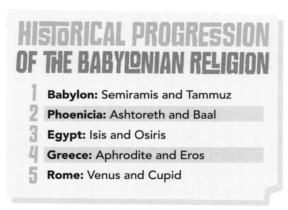

HISTORICAL PROGRESSION OF THE BABYLONIAN RELIGION

1 **Babylon:** Semiramis and Tammuz
2 **Phoenicia:** Ashtoreth and Baal
3 **Egypt:** Isis and Osiris
4 **Greece:** Aphrodite and Eros
5 **Rome:** Venus and Cupid

The subsequent iterations of the pair ended in Rome, but remember, a Roman Empire of sorts (along with all that goes with it) will spring to life at the time of the antichrist. The closer we get to this time, the more stage setting we should expect to see.

Main Views of Mystery Babylon and Babylon the Great

It is clear in Revelation 17 and 18 that John is describing a literal headquarters city (or possibly two cities) for the end-time religious and political Babylonian systems. The question is, what city or cities? There are five candidates that are most often suggested: Jerusalem, New York, Mecca, Rome, and a literal rebuilt Babylon.

Jerusalem doesn't fit the bill because it is not going to be destroyed, but this future Babylon will. The idea of Mecca as the antichrist's headquarters—only recently popularized—does not fit the bill, in my opinion. It has some of the characteristics of Babylon (including idolatry and persecuting God's people), but the religion of Islam does not fit the religious details of what is described in Revelation—it doesn't make sense that Islam would tell the world to worship the beast and his image or anything else other than Allah. Also, I don't see a Muslim figure ever initiating an agreement where Israel would build a temple over or near the Dome of the Rock. This leaves three stronger possibilities: Rome, rebuilt Babylon (in modern-day Iraq), and New York City.

Solid Bible teachers who agree on all other key prophetic end-time details often vary on the identification of Babylon—and I see why that is. It is a complex issue, one that I believe will come into clearer view as we draw closer to the tribulation period. If I can be very honest here, this is an area in which I am still doing a lot of study. I do not yet have a firm conviction on how this will play out. To that end, I have presented the various views for you below.

Literal Rebuilt Babylon

For example, Tim LaHaye, Arnold Fruchtenbaum, and many others believe that a literal rebuilt Babylon in modern-day Iraq will be quickly constructed soon after the rapture (if not before). Their resources teach that the political and religious aspects of the end-times Babylonian system will be based there.

Rome

Dave Hunt, author of *A Woman Rides the Beast*, along with Dr. David Reagan, Bill Salus, Dr. Chuck Missler, and a host of other prophecy experts make a strong case that Rome will be Babylon's future headquarters—particularly for the religious system.

Earlier in Revelation, Jerusalem is referred to as Sodom and Egypt (11:8). So we have a precedent set where a city is given a symbolic name related to the sinful aspects of its history. Supporting this idea further is the fact that in 1 Peter 5:13, Peter was in Rome when he wrote, "She who is in Babylon, chosen together with you, sends you her greetings, and so does my son Mark." Peter used "Babylon" as a code word for Rome.

We are told in verse 9 that the city sits on seven hills. At the time of John's writing, everyone knew this meant Rome. The Roman coins of the time depicted the goddess Roma sitting on seven hills.

Another important clue is found in Revelation 17:6, which reads, "I saw that the woman was drunk with the blood of God's holy people, the blood of those who bore testimony to Jesus." Then we read in Revelation 18:20, "Rejoice, apostles and prophets! For God has judged her with the judgment she imposed on you." These verses seem to be talking about a history of martyring church-age believers, specifically mentioning apostles. At the time of John's writing, he was the only apostle who hadn't yet been killed. Christians were being persecuted and martyred, and this would continue in various forms throughout church history and happens even today.

CHURCH REFORMERS
WHO TAUGHT MYSTERY BABYLON WAS ROME

John Knox, William Tyndale, Martin Luther,
John Calvin, John Wycliffe

EARLY CHURCH LEADERS
WHO TAUGHT MYSTERY BABYLON WAS ROME

Lactantius, Tertullian, Irenaeus, Jerome

As a pagan empire, Rome persecuted Christians, but this persecution continued even when Rome adopted Christian practices. When the Roman emperor Constantine made Christianity legal in AD 313, he merged many aspects of paganism into Christianity. Many of these elements remain in certain forms of Christendom today and will be fully out in the open in the post-rapture world. During the Dark Ages, religious persecution continued in different forms. Examples include the inquisitions and the expulsion of the Jewish people from Spain and Portugal.

America

In his book *Essays in Apocalypse*, author Terry James makes a compelling case for the *possibility* that the headquarters of political Babylon may be located in the United States. Though the nation was built primarily on Christian principles, facilitating religious freedom, and though it has served as a traditional safe haven for the Jewish people as well as the main exporter of missions and the gospel to the world, America has, sadly, also become the chief exporter of abortion, immorality, and culturally corroding media to the world.

Though many Christians are doing their best to serve as salt and light to preserve America's foundational principles, the onslaught of end-times characteristics seem to be building to the point that when the rapture occurs, evil forces will immediately become rampant.

This is the minority view of the three main ones, and those who hold to it say that New York, in particular, is an interesting candidate city if the political Babylon is located in America. The United Nations has its headquarters in New York, and the city is considered by many to be the financial capital of the world.

Rebuilt Babylon

I admire the hearts of those who hold to the literal rebuilt Babylon view because of their high regard for Scripture and their commitment to a literal interpretation of God's Word. They cite details in Isaiah 13, arguing that this chapter has not yet been fulfilled, and say that it describes the tribulation period.

The first 16 verses of Isaiah 13 definitely describe "the day of the LORD" (see verse 6).

THE KINGDOMS
OF DANIEL CHAPTER 2

BABYLON
612 BC

MEDO-PERSIA
539 BC

GREECE
330 BC

ROME
63 BC

DIVIDED KINGDOM
END-TIMES
CONFIGURATION

GOLD SILVER BRONZE IRON IRON&CLAY

This phrase is used in Scripture when prophesying judgment of a nation in the immediate context or during the future tribulation. Sometimes it represents both (see the book of Joel), and sometimes the text switches back and forth between an immediate and distant context, as with the two key descriptions of Satan's fall in Ezekiel (chapter 28) and Isaiah (chapter 14). In both of those cases, the text speaks of contemporary enemy rulers, but clearly shifts—without warning or explanation—to describe the fall of Satan when he rebelled against God and was kicked out of heaven.

When we reach verse 17 in Isaiah 13, we discern a clear shift. A specific people group, the Medes, are mentioned as the enemy that will attack Babylon. Historically, this has already happened. The Babylonian Empire was conquered by the Medo-Persian Empire, which in turn was taken over by the Greek Empire. Then Greece was conquered by Rome.

Due to the fact Isaiah 13 specifically says the Medes were the attackers, I view this chapter as having been fulfilled about 150 years after it was written, when the Medes took Babylon in 539 BC. This, along with the fact that the Babylonian system has morphed and moved through the centuries (and is referred to as a mystery in Revelation 17)—and that the details in John's immediate context clearly point to the Rome of his day—do lend some strength to the idea that the Babylon in view may not be a literal rebuilt Babylon in the modern-day nation of Iraq.

After the Rapture

The false prophet's end-time false religion will, like the antichrist, arise out of— or coalesce in—the area of the ancient Roman Empire. Perhaps after the rapture, when all true Christians are removed from the earth, the false prophet will use the Vatican and other existing church networks and structures throughout Christendom to leverage his false gospel. Perhaps he will be able to amalgamate all world religions into one ecumenical post-rapture New Age religion. There is currently a push in this direction that is becoming prevalent in our day.

QUICK FACT : DID YOU KNOW...

that there is an organization called The World Council of Religious Leaders that works closely with the United Nations in an attempt to unite all world religions?

Modern New Age teaching (which has infiltrated both Catholic and Protestant church circles) affirms that there will come a time when many people will suddenly leave earth. They teach, however, that those who will leave will be purged—they will be unfit for the next level of "evolutionary" and spiritual growth that "Mother Earth" is about to go through. Once again, we see that the enemy knows the future (and believes prophecy) but tries to distort it to fit his evil agenda.

The battleground is in the process of being prepared for this evil end-time religious leader to arise. After the rapture occurs, I believe the false prophet will move quickly onto the scene using existing religious networks and infrastructure. This figure will surely leverage the traditional religious systems and power structures of the world in an updated and thoroughly deceptive way. Through this Mystery Babylon system he will unleash the worst evil ever performed in the name of religion as he causes the world to follow the antichrist and his evil rule.

QUICK FACT: DID YOU KNOW...
that the word *religion* appears only five times in the Bible, and four of those times are negative? James 1:27 is the only positive mention.

If the rapture is coming soon, then this individual may already be on the scene. It's not our job to "pin the tail" on the antichrist or the false prophet, but it is with confidence that we can say the enemy is already at work, filling the world with false teachers, false doctrines, and great deception.

Many evils have been done in the name of religion. Thankfully, those of us who know Christ understand that true Christianity is not a religion, it is a relationship. A true relationship with Jesus never leads people to carry out actions that are not Christlike.

The Collapse of Political Babylon

After reading about the fall of religious Babylon in Revelation 17, we read about the fall of political Babylon in Revelation 18. Any economic system is only as good as the character of the people who take part in it. Here in the United States, people have been blessed with opportunities to succeed financially provided that they are willing to work hard and they are careful to make wise choices. Other countries are not so fortunate. In most developing and underdeveloped nations, there is little to no middle class. You are either rich or absolutely impoverished.

This will be the case during the tribulation period, only the disparity will be on steroids. The principal-less trade system will make many rich—even during the worst time on the planet. Those who buy into the beast's system will get rich off the backs of others. The third seal judgment lets us know that even during famine and economic collapse the rich will still enjoy their life of privilege as the world around them starves to death.

In Revelation 18, we find the global movers and shakers selling everything imaginable—from gold, silver, and jewels to ivory, rare wood, metals, and marble. From expensive wine and olive oil (staples of the rich in biblical literature) to vehicles and human slaves. Human trafficking and slavery will explode during the tribulation period. It's hard to believe conditions will be worse than they are today, but they will be.

HUMAN TRAFFICKING[1]
40.3 MILLION VICTIMS
25% CHILDREN
75% WOMEN AND GIRLS

Revelation 18 tells us the political Babylon will be the economic capital of the world. It will serve as the major hub of all trade, as well as lead the global populace into sin. It will be known as a great city, a global shipping port. Though this Babylon will be mighty in stature, it will suddenly be destroyed by fire (perhaps a nuclear attack), and its collapse will cause global economic ruin and heartache.

This political Babylon will be the seat of government and finance, and its inhabitants will conduct their business and financial pursuits without any link to righteous principles. The sole purpose of all this activity will be to make rich people richer at the expense of others. Not a thought will be given toward any righteous use of money or ethical treatment of people.

Again, some prophecy experts believe that religious and political Babylons represent two entities within the same city, while others say they will have separate locations.

The Main Fact We Need to Know

While there is much discussion about the identities of the religious and political entities in Revelation 17 and 18, there is one fact we can be certain about: The antichrist will turn against the false prophet when he is no longer of use. The global one-world religious leader's seat of power (and possibly even his life) will be destroyed. Then later in the tribulation period, the antichrist's economic and political headquarters will suddenly collapse, causing the greedy and godless global market to collapse like wet cardboard. This will most likely happen toward the end of the tribulation.

As we'll see, these events will set the stage for the people of the world to gather together and attempt to take on God himself. It sounds ludicrous, but in mankind's hard-hearted rebellion, there will be no limit to the extent of foolish self-deception. For those who have received the mark of the beast and seen the ensuing results, fighting God or waiting for him to judge them will be the only options that remain.

CHAPTER 14

The Return of the Warrior-King

After this I heard what sounded like the roar of a great multitude in heaven shouting: "Hallelujah! Salvation and glory and power belong to our God, for true and just are his judgments. He has condemned the great prostitute who corrupted the earth by her adulteries. He has avenged on her the blood of his servants."

REVELATION 19:1-2

We are here.

CHAPTERS

1 2 3 4 5 6 7 8 9 10 11 12 13 14 15 16 17 18 19 20 21 22

PARENTHETICAL CHAPTERS

LETTERS TO THE CHURCHES
CHURCH IN HEAVEN

TRIBULATION PERIOD/FOCUS ON ISRAEL

MILLENNIUM

NEW HEAVEN
NEW EARTH
NEW JERUSALEM

The three-hour movie *Braveheart* chronicles the generational struggle Scotland endured to win her freedom from England. The film is gory and depicts battles as they were—horrific warfare with massive losses of life as generations of Scots fought for freedom with the odds heavily stacked against them. In the movie, freedom wasn't won until after the protagonist William Wallace died a tortuous martyr-like death. At many points in the film, all hope seems lost. But the price Wallace and so many others were willing to pay ultimately led to Scotland winning her freedom. The moment the tide turned toward freedom is depicted at the end of the film, when the rightful king of Scotland, Robert the

Bruce—having been moved by William Wallace's sacrifice—finally leads his country in victorious battle against England.

Braveheart has long been one of my favorite films, and in part I think that is because in many ways, it mirrors biblical history. Generations of God's own have fought the world, the flesh, and the devil—with the odds heavily stacked against them. Evil has proliferated in various times and places in ways that seem unfathomable. God's people have been tortured, enslaved, murdered, and more. At times, all hope has seemed lost, except for two key turning points—the cross and the resurrection! One takes away our sins so we can be right with God again. The other guarantees our victory over death, evil, and the long-laid plans of the enemy who seeks to steal, kill, and destroy.

> John 10:10—The thief does not come except to steal, and to kill, and to destroy. I have come that they may have life, and that they may have it more abundantly (NKJV).

From the prophecy in Genesis 3:15 to the time of the cross, God's promise of a redeemer who would crush the head of the serpent compelled generations of believers to fight on. Since the cross, believers have looked back to that pivotal event to stir their faith and courage, and they now look forward to the day when all of God's promises will be fulfilled. At the cross of Christ, Satan was delivered a fatal blow, but it won't be until the end of the tribulation that his power is fully chained. And it won't be until the end of the millennium (which we'll study in the next chapter) that our enemy will meet his final punishment, when he is thrown into the Lake of Fire for eternity.

The Best Wedding Dinner Ever

Revelation 19 depicts a future victorious moment that eons of the good vs. evil conflict has led up to. All the pain. All the struggles. All the evil done throughout history. In John's future depiction of heaven at the end of the tribulation period, every ounce of evil—embodied and represented in Mystery Babylon the Great—will have collapsed, and heaven will erupt into roaring praise as an amazing event known as the marriage supper of the Lamb takes place!

If you have ever been to a large concert or sporting event, you've experienced the power of a 50,000- to 70,000-seat stadium cheering in unison. Now, imagine that multiplied thousands of times over with every angel and saint in heaven shouting, "Hallelujah!" *Hallelujah* means "praise the Lord." This term is usually spoken in an excited burst of awe-inspired praise for who God is and what he has done.

The word *hallelujah* appears 26 times in Scripture. Four of those instances are in the New Testament, and they are all here in Revelation 19! The remaining 22 uses are all in the Psalms—the Old Testament book of prophecy and praise. It is as if this special word, introduced in the Psalms, will have to await its ultimate usage during this future moment John describes for us in Revelation 19—a moment of all-out celebration!

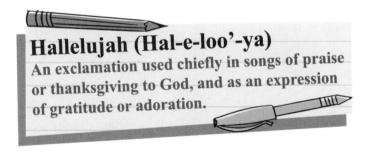

Hallelujah (Hal-e-loo'-ya)
An exclamation used chiefly in songs of praise or thanksgiving to God, and as an expression of gratitude or adoration.

Use your imagination for a moment. If you have accepted Christ as your Savior, you are a cast member in this future event described by John! You will be part of the great multitude, part of the bride of Christ. John used the word *bride* here because the marriage relationship serves as a great illustration of the intimate personal relationship we will have with the Lord. God uses the symbolism of a perfect marriage—unencumbered by sin or struggle—to convey the pure and complete love, peace, joy, and closeness we will experience with our Savior. All believers between Pentecost and the rapture are part of the church and will comprise the bride of Christ.

JEWISH WEDDING TRADITIONS
AND THE RAPTURE

	Jewish Wedding	Spiritual Meaning	
BETROTHAL	LEAVE FATHER'S HOUSE	JESUS LEFT HEAVEN	**1ST COMING OF CHRIST**
	TRAVEL TO DESIRED BRIDE'S HOME	CAME TO EARTH AS A BABY	
	PAY A GREAT PRICE FOR THE BRIDE	DIED ON THE CROSS FOR OUR SINS	
	OFFER ACCEPTED OR REJECTED	OFFERS SALVATION TO US	
	MARRIAGE CONTRACT/LEGALLY BOUND TOGETHER	IF WE ACCEPT WE BECOME THE CHURCH ("BRIDE OF CHRIST")	
	GROOM BACK TO FATHER'S HOUSE TO PREPARE HOME	JESUS WENT BACK TO PREPARE A PLACE FOR US	
WEDDING	FATHER SENDS SON BACK WHEN ALL IS READY	GOD KNOWS THE "DAY AND HOUR" HE WILL SEND THE SON	**RAPTURE AND CHURCH IN HEAVEN DURING TRIBULATION PERIOD**
	GROOMSMEN ANNOUNCE GROOM'S ARRIVAL	THE ARCHANGEL WILL SHOUT AND A TRUMPET WILL BLOW	
	BRIDE IMMEDIATELY TAKEN BACK WITH GROOM	THE CHURCH/BRIDE OF CHRIST WILL BE RAPTURED	
	THE TWO ENTER WEDDING CHAMBER FOR 7 DAYS	THE CHURCH WILL BE IN HEAVEN DURING THE TRIBULATION	
	GREAT WEDDING FEAST AT END OF 7 DAYS	THE CHURCH WILL ATTEND THE WEDDING FEAST OF THE LAMB	

If you know Christ as your Savior, when you read the following verses, I want you to envision yourself as part of this scene. Read it slowly and use your best hi-def, Dolby surround-sound imagination and immerse yourself into this otherworldly moment. If you don't end up with tears or goosebumps, you may need to check your pulse.

Revelation 19:6-9 reads,

> I heard what sounded like a great multitude, like the roar of rushing waters and like loud peals of thunder, shouting: "Hallelujah! For our Lord God Almighty reigns. Let us rejoice and be glad and give him glory! For the wedding of the Lamb has come, and his bride has made herself ready. Fine linen, bright and clean, was given her to wear." (Fine linen stands for the righteous acts of God's holy people.) Then the angel said to me, "Write this: Blessed are those who are invited to the wedding supper of the Lamb!" And he added, "These are the true words of God."

The vast army of heaven is seen here rejoicing at the fall of evil and the commencement of the marriage supper of the Lamb—all in anticipation of the ultimate crescendo event of the ages: the literal, physical return of the Lord Jesus

Christ to Earth. Once again, God himself—the second member of the Trinity—will place his heavenly feet on terra firma in fulfillment of prophecy.

But first, there will be a great celebration and feast! Right now, we—the church—are in the engagement phase of our marriage to Christ. One day soon, he will whisk us away via the rapture and "so we will be with the Lord forever" (1 Thessalonians 4:17). We will be married—united and joined to Christ for all eternity. The wedding supper of the Lamb is the reception. It's the celebration of the marriage and all that it entails.

The Return of the King

Finally, in the closing throes of the tribulation period, with the earth completely ravaged and the sun, moon, and stars blacked out, the blazing glory of the Lord will pierce the sky as he leads the armies of heaven into the earthly realm.

The armies of the world will be gathered for what they think is a war against God, but little do they realize they are preparing themselves as a macabre feast for flesh-eating birds. I'll unpack the chronology of events below, but first, use your God-given imagination to envision this scene—and as you do, envision it from both perspectives.

First, consider the scene from the perspective of the armies gathered on a darkened battle plain. As they stand ready for battle, they witness the might of God's glory suddenly bursting through and illuminating the skies. Second, envision this from the perspective of the armies of heaven (and remember—that includes you if you have accepted Christ as your Savior), who will be gathered behind the Warrior King as part of the most epic procession of all time.

In Revelation 19:11-16, John says,

> I saw heaven standing open and there before me was a white horse, whose rider is called Faithful and True. With justice he judges and wages war. His eyes are like blazing fire, and on his head are many crowns. He has a name written on him that no one knows but he himself. He is dressed in a robe dipped in blood, and his name is the Word of God. The armies of heaven were following him, riding on white horses and dressed in fine linen, white and clean. Coming out of his mouth is a sharp sword with which to strike down the

> nations. "He will rule them with an iron scepter." He treads the winepress of the fury of the wrath of God Almighty. On his robe and on his thigh he has this name written: KING OF KINGS AND LORD OF LORDS.

Little baby Jesus. Meek and mild Jesus. Grace-filled Jesus. Suffering, submissive Jesus. At this guaranteed future moment he will descend as the most powerful and righteous conqueror ever seen by history, heaven, or earth. He is, simply put, King of kings and Lord of lords! Nothing else can even compare.

The Worst Dinner Ever

In Revelation 19:17-21 we read,

> I saw an angel standing in the sun, who cried in a loud voice to all the birds flying in midair, "Come, gather together for the great supper of God, so that you may eat the flesh of kings, generals, and the mighty, of horses and their riders, and the flesh of all people, free and slave, great and small." Then I saw the beast and the kings of the earth and their armies gathered together to wage war against the rider on the horse and his army. But the beast was captured, and with it the false prophet who had performed the signs on its behalf.

With these signs he had deluded those who had received the mark of the beast and worshiped its image. The two of them were thrown alive into the fiery lake of burning sulfur. The rest were killed with the sword coming out of the mouth of the rider on the horse, *and all the birds gorged themselves on their flesh* (emphasis added).

There's a scene you'll never see in a children's picture-book Bible! Those who have produced much of the modern Christian merchandise we have (understandably) toned down some aspects of the Bible. But there are many narratives in Scripture that would be rated R if they were they made into movies. Revelation is definitely among those narratives. Here we see Warrior-King Jesus slaughtering the evil armies of the world simply by speaking some words.

Following the army-destroying shockwaves of Jesus's death speech, we read about a horrific scene that would make Alfred Hitchock's classic film *The Birds* look like a preschool show. The bloody flesh-eating birds feasting on the fallen armies of the world are the complete opposite of the glorious white-linen wedding supper in heaven. The contrast is stark, vivid, and very intentional. Mercy has run its course. Grace has been all used up. It will be time for evil to meet its deserved punishment.

Order of Events

Just as we observed that a cluster of key mid-tribulation events were highlighted in the parenthetical chapters of Revelation 10–14, we also find a cluster of key events occurring at the end of the tribulation period. During the entire tribulation, there will be so much happening so fast that it will be difficult to keep up. Some details John provides are single events, some are ongoing developments, and still others layer on top of each other. So, it's difficult to put together an exact

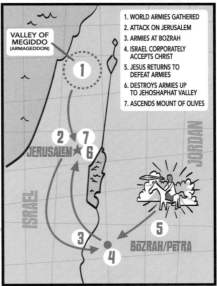

CAMPAIGN OF
ARMAGEDDON

VALLEY OF MEGIDDO (ARMAGEDDON)

1. WORLD ARMIES GATHERED
2. ATTACK ON JERUSALEM
3. ARMIES AT BOZRAH
4. ISRAEL CORPORATELY ACCEPTS CHRIST
5. JESUS RETURNS TO DEFEAT ARMIES
6. DESTROYS ARMIES UP TO JEHOSHAPHAT VALLEY
7. ASCENDS MOUNT OF OLIVES

JERUSALEM
ISRAEL
JORDAN
BOZRAH/PETRA

chronological order of events, but with a careful study of all prophetic scriptures, a timeline of events will emerge. While we can't be dogmatic about every detail (nor should we), we can construct a basic timeline using logic and by comparing scripture with scripture.

With that said, for clarity's sake, here is the basic order of the events that will take place during the closing portion of the tribulation period. Some events (such as those related to establishing the millennial kingdom) will be covered in more detail in the following chapters.

Clean Clothes and Heavenly Olympics

As we think about the glorious events described in Revelation 19, there's something I want to point out from the verses above. Note that the fine linen stands for the righteous acts that we do. We are saved by grace—salvation is a free gift that we cannot earn. But we are saved unto good works. The book of James powerfully details how our actions demonstrate the existence of our faith within. Real faith plays out in real action.

> James 2:26—As the body without the spirit is dead, so faith without deeds is dead.

In preparation for our privileged return with Christ along with the armies of heaven, there's another amazing event that will precede that moment. Scripture indicates that while we are in heaven and the tribulation is taking place on earth, the church will stand before the judgment seat of Christ—also known as the Bema Seat Judgment. It will be as if we were standing on the awards platform after an Olympic finals event. At this judgment seat our salvation will not be in question at all, but our works will be evaluated and we will be given eternal rewards.

The thought of the Bema Seat

Judgment and this moment depicted in Revelation 19 should light a fire under each of us who know Christ to work hard for the Lord in this life. We won't regret going all-out for him. Again, we don't work *for* our salvation, but good works should definitely result *from* our salvation. When a complete stranger gets you off of death row by taking your place, it should result in a close bond and a life of action that is lived out of sheer thankfulness and dedication.

My son who is in college now had the opportunity to attend school part-time during his junior and senior years in high school because he had already fulfilled some of what was required for graduation. We encouraged him to take AP and college-level courses to fill up the time. At first he wrestled with that idea; then he embraced it and worked hard. The payoff came later when he started college with existing class credits, which allowed him to save time and money. Once enrolled in college, he was extremely glad he had put in the hard work earlier.

When you and I sacrifice for the Lord and give of our time, money, emotions, blood, sweat, and tears to invest in the Lord's work, we can look forward to some amazing rewards. We will also have some regrets—we will all realize we missed some opportunities we could have leveraged for the Lord's glory.

Let the thought of standing before Christ in the future drive your present actions. Don't give up on your marriage. Don't walk away from that ministry. Don't stop investing in your children, friendships, local church. Serve those whom the world overlooks. Meet the needs of those who can never pay you back. Do the hard things now. I promise—you won't regret it later!

In fact, the rewards we are given at the Bema Seat will determine our roles in Christ's future millennial kingdom! Turn the page, and we'll explore what that is all about.

CHAPTER 15

A Literal 1,000-Year Utopia

This, then, is how you should pray: "Our Father in heaven, hallowed be your name, your kingdom come, your will be done, on earth as it is in heaven."

MATTHEW 6:9-10

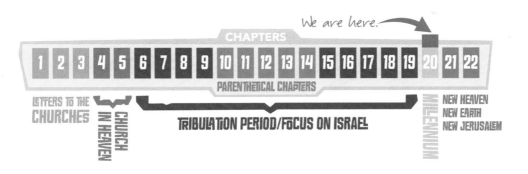

We are here.

CHAPTERS

1 2 3 4 5 6 7 8 9 10 11 12 13 14 15 16 17 18 19 20 21 22

PARENTHETICAL CHAPTERS

LETTERS TO THE CHURCHES — CHURCH IN HEAVEN — TRIBULATION PERIOD/FOCUS ON ISRAEL — MILLENNIUM — NEW HEAVEN NEW EARTH NEW JERUSALEM

We often quote the Lord's prayer without thinking much about the words. It's easy for us, once we committed something to memory, to simply recite it as if we were saying the pledge of allegiance or uttering a memorized dinner or bed-time prayer. We can easily overlook the clear meaning of something when we're able to quote it from memory without thinking very deeply about what we're saying. We also tend to forget that the Lord's prayer is a *prayer*, not a statement. Through the Lord's prayer we are asking God for specific things to happen.

Keep in mind that God always answers prayer. Sometimes his answer is yes. Other times it is no. Still others it is not yet. I'd like for us to note one key detail in the prayer that Jesus modeled for us that the church has been praying for 2,000 years. God's answer to this prayer—prayed billions of times by millions of Christians—has been, and continues to be, "Not yet." It has a specific time stamp. Other events must take place first before this specific prayer is answered.

There is a sense in which God's kingdom is already here (through his church, and before that, through Old Testament believers). I address that in more detail below, but what we need to remember is that Jesus modeled a prayer that requests God's kingdom to come in such a way that God's will—God's righteous reign—is carried out on earth "as it is in heaven."

The last time I checked, God's will was accomplished 100 percent of the time in heaven. Also, the last time I checked (just a few minutes ago on the news), we live in a fallen, evil world where atrocities, terror attacks, mass shootings, corruption, human trafficking, and child abuse still occur. When Jesus prayed for God's will to be done on earth as it is in heaven, he was referring to a literal future kingdom that has long been prophesied by the Old Testament prophets.

When Jesus took a donkey ride into Jerusalem on what we refer to as the triumphal entry or Palm Sunday, the Jewish people were fully expecting him to establish a literal earthly kingdom. They wanted to see oppressive Rome overthrown and kicked out of Israel. What they didn't understand at the time was the mystery of the church age—God's plan to reach the entire world had to occur first. Their view of the expected kingdom was merely political in nature. But God had so much more in store. At the end of the tribulation, God's "Not yet" answer will finally turn into a glorious, over-the-top "Yes!"

A Literal 1,000 Years

There are three primary views about the millennial kingdom. The only view that employs a literal interpretation method, and rejects allegorizing or spiritualizing the text, is the premillennial view. I covered the interpretation methods of the main views of the millennium in depth in my book *The Non-Prophet's Guide™ to the End Times*. Assuming you are convinced that a literal, futurist interpretation of Revelation is the correct way to handle the

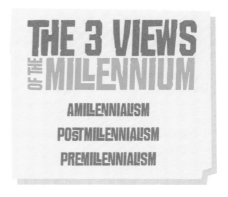

text, the plain reading leads us to conclude that John is describing a literal 1,000-year period that is still future. There are many Old and New Testament prophecies (discussed below) that necessitate this be a literal period that's still to come.

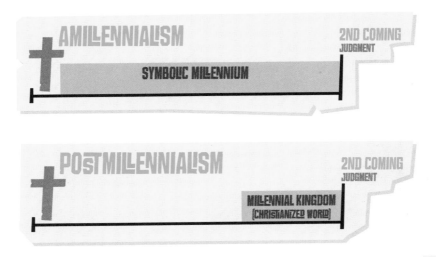

One of the arguments used to support the amillennial or postmillennial views is that Jesus taught the kingdom of God is within the believer (Luke 17:20-21), and that the kingdom of God is at hand, or near (Matthew 3:2; 4:17; Mark 1:15).

There is definitely a sense in which the kingdom of God is on Earth today residing with the church—that is, every true believer in Christ. This is evident by several of Jesus's statements. But what we find in Scripture is that in each distinct era of God's activity in human history, he had a form of his kingdom on earth. For example, we find verses in the Old Testament indicating that God's kingdom was expressed through the nation of Israel, such as Exodus 19:6.

It's also true that the kingdom of God was at hand—meaning that if the Jewish religious leaders and the nation as a whole would have received their Messiah at the time, the kingdom would have been instituted. Jesus was brokenhearted over their rejection because he knew that meant the kingdom could not be instituted and that Israel would have to go through horrific times (through church history and during the tribulation) before she would finally accept him as their long-awaited Messiah.

Toward the end of his earthly ministry, when it was clear that the religious leaders would reject Jesus and continue to lead the people of Israel astray, Jesus said in Matthew 23:37-39,

Jerusalem, Jerusalem, you who kill the prophets and stone those sent to you, how often I have longed to gather your children together, as a hen gathers her chicks under her wings, and you were not willing. Look, your house is left to you desolate. For I tell you, you will not see me again until you say, "Blessed is he who comes in the name of the Lord."

With this statement Jesus prophesied that their rejection would lead to their desolation. But at a future time—at the very end of the tribulation—they will finally, fully, corporately see that he was indeed their Messiah. Paul affirms this as well in Romans chapters 9–11, which is summed up succinctly in Romans 11:26, where he says, "All Israel will be saved."

For sure, there is a paradox present here. God is all-knowing and knew Israel would reject Jesus at his first coming. But somehow, in a very real sense, if they would have received him, the kingdom of God would have been instituted at his first coming. Don't try to reconcile these facts in your head. There is an inherent paradox in many key theological concepts.

Par•a•dox = something that seems like a
noun   contradiction but is true

For example, Jesus was fully God and fully man. We live our Christian life, but Christ lives it through us. God is three in one. God is completely sovereign, but at the same time we have free will. The corporate rejection of the Messiah at Jesus's first coming kept the kingdom from arriving in full. But at the same time, God knew this rejection would lead to the church age and the salvation of countless Gentiles. We are not God, so we can't reconcile these mysteries. We must simply accept that he is God and we are not.

Also, recall that Revelation is all about the ultimate culmination and resolution of every key biblical theme. This is also true when it comes to the kingdom. We live in a fallen world ruled by Satan, but within this setting the kingdom of heaven grows with every new believer who accepts Christ as Savior. One day God will bring all aspects of his kingdom promises together (including Old Testament believers coreigning with church age believers) into a future earthly kingdom.

As we study Scripture, we find that there are many Old and New Testament prophecies that specifically refer to the future literal kingdom on earth. Consider the chart on the next page.

A FEW OF THE MANY VERSES DETAILING LITERAL FUTURE KINGDOM

OLD TESTAMENT
- Exodus 19:6
- Isaiah 2:2
- Isaiah 9:6-7
- Isaiah 24:23
- Isaiah 42:3-4
- Daniel 7:18, 27
- Zechariah 14:1-9

NEW TESTAMENT
- Matthew 8:11
- Luke 22:28-30
- Acts 1:6-7
- Acts 14:22
- 1 Corinthians 6:9
- 2 Timothy 2:12
- 2 Peter 1:11

As we consider all of the above, it gives us solid footing to resist allegorizing the clear and plain sense of John's description of a 1,000-year reign of Christ. Just to make sure we didn't miss the point, he mentions the 1,000-year time period six times in just seven verses. In Revelation 20:1-7 we read,

> I saw an angel coming down out of heaven, having the key to the Abyss and holding in his hand a great chain. He seized the dragon, that ancient serpent, who is the devil, or Satan, and bound him for a *thousand years*. He threw him into the Abyss, and locked and sealed it over him, to keep him from deceiving the nations anymore until the *thousand years* were ended. After that, he must be set free for a short time.
>
> I saw thrones on which were seated those who had been given authority to judge. And I saw the souls of those who had been beheaded because of their testimony about Jesus and because of the word of God. They had not worshiped the beast or its image and had not received its mark on their foreheads or their hands. They came to life and reigned with Christ a *thousand years*. (The rest of the dead did not come to life until the *thousand years* were ended.) This is the first resurrection. Blessed and holy are those who share in the first resurrection. The second death has no power over them, but they will be priests of God and of Christ and will reign with him for a *thousand years*. When the *thousand years* are over, Satan will be released from his prison (emphasis added).

The plain sense of this passage informs us that the 1,000 years described by John will take place after tribulation-era believers will have refused to accept the mark of the beast. It also tells us that Satan will be bound during the 1,000-year period. If Satan's 1,000-year imprisonment in the abyss is merely allegorical, then Satan must have a pretty long chain based on all the evil he has done throughout the church age.

QUICK FACT: DID YOU KNOW...

that the Greek word for 1,000, *chilioi* (khil'-ee-oy), means (drumroll please)...1,000?

Life in the Millennial Kingdom

I can recall the first time I heard about the millennial kingdom. This concept seemed strange to me. In my mind, it made more sense to keep things simple. If I were God, I would take care of all the "final things" at the same time—judge evil, take all believers to heaven, and live happily ever after in the eternal state. But I'm not God. God has a specific purpose for everything he does. Three of the main purposes for the millennial kingdom are (1) to fulfill prophecy, (2) to provide a time period for God's children to rule alongside Christ with righteousness, and (3) to prove once and for all that sin is not a product of our environment but our nature.

All that said, what will life be like during the millennial kingdom? Does the Bible shed light on this? Yes, it does—quite a lot.

People

At the end of the tribulation period there will be some believers who survived, including the 144,000 Jewish evangelists, the remnant of Jewish Christians whom Jesus rescues upon his return, and possibly other believers who somehow make it to the end of the tribulation. These believers will repopulate the world once the millennial kingdom is established (Isaiah 65:23). Their life spans will be longer than today—similar to the life spans of those who lived during the pre-Flood era (Isaiah 65:20). Though they will start strong, as the earth is repopulated, not all of their descendants will accept Christ as Savior, even though he will be literally ruling the world with perfect righteousness. It is these unbelieving descendants who will join forces with Satan at the end of the millennium to battle against God (Revelation 20:7-9).

Those of us who are caught up in the rapture will spend seven years with the Lord in heaven, return with him, and serve him in the millennial kingdom. We will enter the kingdom with the glorified spiritual bodies that are given to us at the rapture/resurrection. We (like the angels) will not be married or even have a desire to be married (Matthew 22:30; Mark 12:25). We will help the Lord govern the world in its new state (Luke 22:30; 1 Thessalonians 4:13-18; Revelation 5:10). This next detail is truly amazing to me: Old Testament-era believers will be raised from the dead at the beginning of the millennium, and we church-age believers will partner with them as we rule with Jesus (Isaiah 26:19; Ezekiel 37:13-14; Daniel 12:1-2)! More on this below.

Animals

If you've ever studied the animal world, or if you have watched any nature documentaries about life in the wild, you've surely seen how brutal and unforgiving the animal kingdom is. This was not the original state of the world or God's intention when he created everything. Adam and Eve's fall into sin corrupted the entire creation. This aspect of the curse will be removed during the millennial kingdom, and you'll be happy to know there will be no carnivores or poisonous animals in the future kingdom. No animals will ever want to eat or attack you. The earth will be returned to the conditions that existed before the fall (Isaiah 11:6-9).

Earth

Along with the animal kingdom living at peace, the earth as a whole will be renovated. Humankind and nature will live harmoniously as originally intended (Isaiah 2:2; 11:6-9; Zechariah 14:8), and the geography of the world will change for the better. Jerusalem—the historical epicenter of God's prophecies and activity—will become the highest point on earth.

I'm looking forward to a world with no poison ivy, thorns, ticks, or mosquitoes! If the last two still exist in the kingdom, I'm sure they will only bite plants!

Government

During the millennium, Jesus will rule the entire world—which is what sin-filled rulers have tried to do all through human history. Christ, however, will reign with righteousness. Evil figures throughout history, from Nimrod to Hitler to the future antichrist, are all marked by aspirations to rule the entire world. Ultimately, all will have failed and will leave carnage and destruction in their wake. One day, however, the rightful King will sit on earth's throne in Jerusalem and govern with complete righteousness (Isaiah 9:7; 33:22; Jeremiah 23:5; Matthew 19:28; 25:31; 1 Timothy 6:15; Revelation 17:14; 20:4).

Church-age believers, along with Old Testament believers, will help Jesus rule the nations (Revelation 2:26-27; 20:4), judge the world (1 Corinthians 6:2), and will be "a chosen people, a royal priesthood, a holy nation" (1 Peter 2:9). Some expositors suggest that we will be given more or less authority and responsibility in the millennial kingdom depending on how we managed the opportunities and responsibilities we had while we lived in our natural state (Luke 19:11-27).

Satan's Head Finally Crushed

At this time, you and I do not fully realize why Satan's reign has been allowed to linger, why God's judgment against him has not been swift and immediate, and why Satan will only be chained instead of destroyed after the tribulation

period. Remember, God has a purpose for everything he does, and for now, we see things very dimly (1 Corinthians 13:12 NKJV). We don't yet see how all the details connect. But rest assured, Satan will get what is coming to him.

We read this in Revelation 20:7-10:

> When the thousand years are over, Satan will be released from his prison and will go out to deceive the nations in the four corners of the earth—Gog and Magog—and to gather them for battle. In number they are like the sand on the seashore. They marched across the breadth of the earth and surrounded the camp of God's people, the city he loves. But fire came down from heaven and devoured them. And the devil, who deceived them, was thrown into the lake of burning sulfur, where the beast and the false prophet had been thrown. They will be tormented day and night for ever and ever.

There are a few key points to observe here. First, in short order upon his release, Satan will be able to deceive the nations into one last rebellion—proving once again that we as humans are responsible for our own sin and can't say, "The devil made me do it." Those who are born to the believers who survive the tribulation and enter into the millennial kingdom will still have a sin nature, and not all will accept Christ and follow his ways. By the end of the 1,000 years, there will be many unbelievers who are willing to rebel against Christ, and when Satan is released, he will gather them for one last battle. This will demonstrate once and for all that mankind's sin nature is enough to cause people to rebel against God—even in a perfect utopia.

Second, Gog and Magog are mentioned again. This is not the same pre-tribulation or early-tribulation war we studied earlier in this book, but an iconic reference to it. It is similar to how people symbolically reference famous battles or wars today. The famous battle of Waterloo, for example, has been used as an idiom to represent a tough struggle. Another example is how people use the terms *Armageddon* and *apocalypse* to mean destruction. Neither term actually means destruction, but the connotations are understood.

Third, once again—for the last time—the world's attention and aggression will focus on Jerusalem. If these future rebels won't believe the accounts of Jesus wrecking shop at the second coming simply by speaking a word, then they will learn firsthand that righteous-ruling Jesus can and will put the supernatural smackdown on open rebellion. As soon as the hordes in this final rebellion finish their long trek and surround Jerusalem, fire will come down and instantly vaporize them.

Fourth, Satan will finally be cast into the lake of burning sulfur, never to escape. In other words, evil will not merely be destroyed, it will be eternally punished. The beast and the false prophet, who were thrown into the lake 1,000 years earlier, are seen still existing in this horrible place.

The dragon. The serpent. The devil. The accuser. The thief. The destroyer. These and many other names describe the figure who has caused so much pain and destruction throughout history. He will finally be completely and utterly punished—permanently. We're so used to evil being part of the equation that it is difficult to fully realize the weight of what this will mean.

The Scariest Passage of Scripture

Some people shudder when they read the biblical accounts of demon possession, graphically depicted battles, or intimidating giants. Of all the passages of Scripture, Revelation 20:11-15 scares me the most. Not because it applies to me, but because it applies to everyone who has rejected God. Imagine the moment when God's only recourse is to be fair. That might not sound scary, but it is. All through history, God has offered grace, mercy, and forgiveness. In fact, he went so far as to die a tortuous death in our place so we could avoid getting what we deserve.

Here's what I mean: We either get what is fair—and pay for our own sins—or we receive God's grace and forgiveness. But grace and forgiveness are found only when we accept God's gracious offer. The cross is a scandal. Who else lets people off the hook and pays the price for it with their very own life? Yet many reject this offer.

I don't know all the intricacies of how, when, and why people are responsible for rejecting Christ, but God does. And after every possible avenue is exhausted to give people time to repent and turn to the Savior, the inevitable must come. After the millennial kingdom, the final rebellion, and Satan's ultimate judgment, we read about a future event in which all unbelievers will stand before God to answer for their sins.

We read about this event in Revelation 20:11-15, where John describes what he saw with these words:

> I saw a great white throne and him who was seated on it. The earth and the heavens fled from his presence, and there was no place for them. And I saw the dead, great and small, standing before the throne, and books were opened. Another book was opened, which is the book of life. The dead were judged according to what they had done as recorded in the books. The sea gave up the dead that were in it, and death and Hades gave up the dead that were in them, and each person was judged according to what they had done. Then death and Hades were thrown into the lake of fire. The lake of fire is the second death. Anyone whose name was not found written in the book of life was thrown into the lake of fire.

In this amazing scene we see everything fade away except the throne and the books. Are these books literal volumes, or are they some kind of heavenly databank? The Greek word used here for books is *biblos* (βίβλος) and it refers to a sacred or super-natural scroll, book, or volume. It is a supernaturally kept volume of data on each person who has ever lived. If you think the data centers that governments and trans-national data companies have are big, think about the amount of data God has kept through the ages! Every thought, action, motive, and word of every person who has ever existed has been kept in God's supernatural library of "books."

Notice also John mentions that the Lake of Fire is "the second death" (Revelation 20:14). In Scripture, we learn that there are two births and two deaths. Natural birth refers to when we are physically born, and spiritual birth takes place when we accept Christ as Savior (John 3:3-6). Natural death occurs when our physical bodies die, and the second death, which is spiritual, will happen when people are thrown into the Lake of Fire. So if you are born twice you die once, but if you are born once, you die twice.

There are also two resurrections. This confuses some people because we find more than two resurrections in the Bible (for example, church-age believers will be resurrected at the rapture, and Old Testament believers will be resurrected before the millennial kingdom). But Scripture reveals that ultimately there are two types of resurrections: a believer's resurrection and an unbeliever's resurrection. There are multiple believers' resurrections, but only one unbelievers' resurrection—described here by John in Revelation 20.

A New Perspective

Thinking about our glorious future is almost overwhelming. Our minds can barely handle the thought of what is in store for us. Indeed, we have a lot to look forward to in this literal 1,000-year kingdom in which we will rule with Christ. Some have argued that we shouldn't focus too much on our promised future. They say, "We don't want to become so heavenly minded that we are no earthly good."

I have found the opposite to be true. The more I study the reality of what is in store for us, the more awe I have for my Creator and Savior. This awe leads to devotion and dedication that positively influences my actions toward others.

I have met some people who are content with gaining head knowledge from the Bible but never allowing that knowledge to flow to their heart and ultimately to their hands and feet. These kinds of people get caught in the minutiae of actionless academic Bible study. But if we allow our imaginations to take hold of what John has described, and if we let our unmerited salvation take hold of our hearts, then contemplating these amazing future events should lead us to concrete actions that enable us to function as salt and light in a decaying and darkening world.

Thinking about our future stretches our perspective. It provides a broader view of what God is doing in us and through us. I believe our current discipleship is preparing us not just for this life, but our service in the millennial kingdom and beyond. What if the interests, skills, personality, challenges, relationships, and spiritual gifts you currently possess are all preparing you for your future service in the millennial kingdom? Doesn't that thought change your perspective for the better?

For those of us who know the Lord, let's commit now to letting him have his way in our lives. When that prospect gets difficult, let's focus on our amazing future and allow that to dictate how we live today. Our future should not distract us from living today, it should guide how we live today.

For those who do not yet know the Lord—please accept his free gift of salvation today while you have the opportunity. If accepting Christ is something you want to do, here's how. It's very simple, but people often make it too complex. One does not become a Christian by following a formula, but I've found that what I'm about to share is an effective way to explain what it means to receive Christ and become a true Christian. It's so simple a child can understand it. It's as simple as A, B, C.

Admit that you are a sinner. No one is perfect. We all fall short. Romans 3:23: "All have sinned and fall short of the glory of God." Romans 6:23: "The wages [payment] of sin is death, but the gift of God is eternal life in Christ Jesus our Lord."

Believe that Jesus is God's Son and that he died on the cross with your sins on him. Romans 5:8: "While we were still sinners, Christ died for us."

Confess him as your Lord. This doesn't mean you will never mess up again. Rather, it means you will serve him and learn his ways as you grow spiritually. Romans 10:9 (NKJV): "If you confess with your mouth the Lord Jesus and believe in your heart that God has raised Him from the dead, you will be saved." You can use the following prayer as a guide for what to say:

> "Lord Jesus, I admit that I am a sinner. I have sinned against you, and sin separates me from you. I thank you that you died on the cross for me. You took my sins upon you and paid my penalty at the cross. I believe you are who you say you are—God in the flesh. I believe you died for my sins. I want to accept your gift of salvation and, at this moment, I ask you to be my Savior. I thank you for this great forgiveness. I now have new life. I now claim you as my Savior and my Lord. In Jesus's name, amen."

The Alternative

The Lake of Fire (whatever that actually is) does not sound like a good prospect. It seems extreme to our fallen human sensibilities, but somehow it is the necessary residence and logical outcome for those who are judged based on how they lived. I do believe there are degrees of punishment in eternity (see Luke 10; Luke 12:47-48; Revelation 20:12). Aside from that, we don't know the details, but God has given all of us (Romans 1:18-20) enough warning to avoid it altogether! We can bank on this: God is completely fair. When all is said and done, even those separated from God in eternity will not question whether they deserve their punishment.

fair•ness = impartial and just treatment or behavior without favoritism or discrimination
noun

As amazing as the millennial kingdom is going to be, we're not done yet! Remarkably, after the millennial kingdom will come a phase known as the eternal state. We'll take a close look at that in the next chapter.

CHAPTER 16

Creation Renovation

I saw "a new heaven and a new earth," for the first heaven and the first earth had passed away.

REVELATION 21:1

Over the years I've had the opportunity to go on a few short-term mission trips. Each trip has had moments of excitement, adventure, team-building, and worship. Each one has also had moments of struggle, discomfort, exhaustion, heartbreak, and homesickness. When you go on such trips, you discover that because everyone in the group shares the same experiences and goals, you develop a bond as a team, as well as bond with other individuals. Together you understand, experientially, what the adventure has been like.

Each trip has had many unique aspects to it, but all of them had one thing in common: the struggle to adequately describe the experience to others upon returning home. After being immersed in the sights, sounds, smells, and movements of the Holy Spirit and attacks from the enemy, it is very difficult to convey all that information to someone who wasn't there. As you talk to others or attempt to put together a mission trip report, you find that your best attempts

WISH YOU WERE HERE.

to describe what happened pales in comparison to what you experienced. The same is true for adventures like skydiving, or scuba diving, or visiting a spectacular national park or famous landmark.

At the time of this writing I have yet to visit Israel, but I have talked to many people who have been there. They all share the same sentiment. Believers who have gone to Israel tell me that you simply can't put the experience into words. They say it is utterly indescribable to walk where Jesus walked, to see the actual places we read about in the Old and New Testaments, and to ponder the prophesied future events that are on the near horizon.

As we near the finish line in our study of Revelation, we transition from John's description of the millennial kingdom in Revelation 20 to what he recorded next about the new heaven and new earth in Revelation 21. This final environment in which we'll live—also referred to as the *eternal state*—is beyond describing!

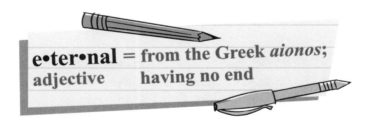

e•ter•nal = from the Greek *aionos*; adjective   having no end

John did his best throughout Revelation to describe what he saw and experienced. He had a front-row seat to the supernatural, to technology that was light-years beyond anything he had ever seen, and to destruction on a level that nobody other than God had previously known. The judgments of the tribulation period were difficult for John to describe. Then what he saw of the millennial kingdom posed an entirely new challenge. How could he best explain what he was seeing? And finally, as he wrote Revelation 21 and 22, John had the ultimate challenge: describing the eternal state—the final and perfect level of existence we as believers will experience.

I find it interesting that John used 16 chapters to describe the 7-year tribulation period, but only 1 chapter for the 1,000-year millennial kingdom and less than 2 chapters for the eternal state—which will last forever. I believe a key part of the reason for this is that John simply could not adequately describe what he saw, nor could he fully comprehend much of it. Based on the glimpse we get in Revelation 21–22, it appears the eternal state will be so otherworldly that most of its attributes are beyond describing. It's not a stretch to imagine that there will be colors, sights, sounds, smells, physics, and experiences that we can't currently comprehend with our limited thinking and in our mortal bodies.

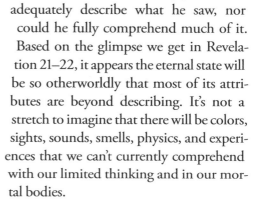

In 2 Corinthians 12:4, Paul described a time when he was "caught up" to the third heaven and witnessed things that were so glorious, so amazing, so mind-blowing that he was not even allowed to share what he witnessed! Earlier, in Paul's first letter to the Corinthians, he wrote, "Eye has not seen, nor ear heard, nor have entered in the heart of man the things which God has prepared for those who love Him" (1 Corinthians 2:9 NKJV).

Rather than attempt to explain everything he experienced, John spends more time in Revelation 21 describing what will *not* be in the eternal state. No more death. No more pain. No more suffering. No more tears. No more relational breakdown. We also find there will be no sea. Seas separate people. Any type of separation will be a thing of the past. Every race, tribe, tongue, and people group will live in perfect unity and community with each other and with the Lord.

Heaven is mentioned in the Bible 532 times, and more than 10 percent of those are in Revelation! John speaks of heaven no less than 55 times. It is a real place in an unseen realm outside of our space-time continuum. But it is not ethereal. We do not become "one with the universe" or float around as wispy, bodiless spirits. We will maintain our identities. We will still have the glorified spiritual bodies that we will receive at the rapture. We will still be us, only much better, and we will be living in perfect unity with God and others. I'm sure if we caught a glimpse of what Paul or John saw, we, too, would be short on words.

A New Jerusalem—The Eternal Capital City

The crowning feature of the new heaven and the new earth will be its capital city, the New Jerusalem. Throughout Scripture, Jerusalem has played a key role in God's unfolding story. It only makes sense that this key city—the one that herni-

ates the backs of those who try to move its borders (Zechariah 12:3) and the one that God calls the apple of his own eye (Zechariah 2:8)—would receive such immense glory and attention in the eternal state along with the new heaven and new earth.

The Bible speaks of Jerusalem as the center of the nations. Indeed, it is the historical crossroads of Europe, Asia, and Africa. As an interesting aside, most languages to the east of Jerusalem are written from right to left, while most languages west of Jerusalem are written from left to right. Trade routes and languages all seem to point to

Jerusalem. Whenever Scripture gives a direction (north, south, east, west), it is in relation to Jerusalem.

In addition to being the geographical and linguistic center of the world, Jerusalem has also been the center of at least 36 wars and is considered the epicenter of Bible prophecy. The destruction of Jerusalem in AD 70 was prophesied by Daniel (chapter 9) and by Jesus in the Olivet Discourse (Matthew 24; Mark 13; and Luke 21). Luke 21:24 informs us that Jerusalem would remain out of the hands of the Jewish people "until the times of the Gentiles are fulfilled."

In 1948, Israel became a nation again in a single day (exactly as foretold in Isaiah 66:8). In 1967, Israel once again controlled Jerusalem as a result of the Six-Day War. And today, the nations of the world (via the UN) are obsessed with Israel and Jerusalem, just as prophesied in Zechariah 12:3. Apparently "the times of the Gentiles" is transitioning to set the stage for all end-time events to take place.

This central location theme of Bible prophecy finds its full resolution in Revelation. John provided us with the first few details about the New Jerusalem in Revelation 21:2, where he wrote, "I saw the Holy City, the new Jerusalem, coming down out of heaven from God, prepared as a bride beautifully dressed for her husband." Then John wrote several more specifics about the city in verses 9-27, and some final details in Revelation 22:1-5.

The most descriptive section is found in 21:16-21. I highly recommend you carefully and slowly read the entire chapter for context, but I've included those few verses here just to give you a taste of the absolute beauty of this greatest of all cities. There we read,

> The city was laid out like a square, as long as it was wide. He measured the city with the rod and found it to be 12,000 stadia in length, and as wide and high as it is long. The angel measured the wall using human measurement, and it was 144 cubits thick. The wall was made of jasper, and the city of pure gold, as pure as glass. The foundations of the city walls were decorated with every kind of precious

stone. The first foundation was jasper, the second sapphire, the third agate, the fourth emerald, the fifth onyx, the sixth ruby, the seventh chrysolite, the eighth beryl, the ninth topaz, the tenth turquoise, the eleventh jacinth, and the twelfth amethyst. The twelve gates were twelve pearls, each gate made of a single pearl. The great street of the city was of gold, as pure as transparent glass.

We are told here that the new Jerusalem will be a 1,380-mile (in each direction) cube coming from heaven to earth in glorious fashion. To give you an idea of its size, this immense city is slightly smaller than our moon. It would stretch from Florida to Maine and would be 150,000 times the size of London, currently the world's largest geographical city. Will this city rest on earth? Will it hover? Will it orbit the earth? We are not told, but one day we will find out.

Notice that the city will exist prior to the eternal state. It will come down out of heaven and will be presented in some fashion. Other passages of Scripture provide additional hints about the New Jerusalem, and many Bible teachers believe it already exists and is what Jesus was referring to in John 14:2 when he said, "My Father's house has many rooms; if that were not so, would I have told you that I am going there to prepare a place for you?"

It's also the city spoken of in Hebrews 11:10, where we read that Abraham "was looking forward to the city with foundations, whose architect and builder is God." Then in Hebrews 13:14 we are told, "Here we do not have an enduring city, but we are looking for the city that is to come."

INTERESTING FACTS
ABOUT THE NEW JERUSALEM

HEIGHT, WIDTH, DEPTH

1,380 miles each direction

CUBE VS. PYRAMID

Pyramids associated with occult and sun worship
Cube associated with God's presence/temple/Holy of Holies

FUNCTIONAL CONSTRUCTION

Resurrected bodies not subject to gravity
"Streets" may include vertical passageways
City "blocks" may be cubes as well
The city will match how bodies function

CAPACITY

The New Jerusalem could house 20 billion people
averaging 75 acres per person (still only using 25% of the city)

Calculations taken from *The Revelation Record* by Dr. Henry Morris
(Carol Stream, IL: Tyndale House Publishers, 1983), 450-451.

Jesus has been building this city for almost 2,000 years—adding "mansions" (as some translations render John 14:2) for each person who accepts Christ. If our Lord created the entire present universe in 6 days, I can only imagine what the New Jerusalem will be like given that it has been almost 2,000 years in the making!

In Revelation 21–22, we learn that this city of God will be covered in jewels and precious stones of every kind—more pure than anything we've ever seen. God will have his throne there, and his glory will be the source of the city's never-ending light. God's presence in Scripture is often seen as brilliant light. In the New Jerusalem, the glory of God's presence will burst forth in unlimited radiating brilliance and will be reflected throughout the heavenly jeweled city in a dazzling display of refracting colors.

The city will have 12 gates, each made of a single pearl and eternally linked to the 12 tribes of Israel. The New Jerusalem will also be built on 12 solid

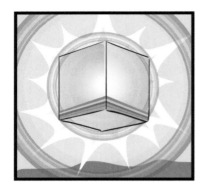

foundations—eternally linked to and named after the apostles, whom we are told are the foundation of the church (Ephesians 2:20). The makeup of the city will be a constant reminder of the unity of Old and New Testament saints of every tribe, nation, tongue, and people.

Heaven's "main street" will be made of pure, clear gold and a river will flow from the throne room of God right down the middle of the street. Angels will stand at the gates and the city will be populated by God's redeemed children. The New Jerusalem—the capital city of eternity—will serve as a perpetual reminder of God's redemptive plan through the ages. And we will call this place home!

GENESIS — REVELATION

GENESIS	REVELATION
BANISHED FROM GOD'S PRESENCE	LIVE WITH GOD FOREVER
TREE OF LIFE OFF LIMITS	ACCESS TO TREE OF LIFE
EARTH CURSED	CURSE REMOVED
ANIMALS EAT EACH OTHER	ANIMALS HERBIVORES

Home

I often find myself in a hotel room due to business trips, mission trips, travel for my kids' soccer games, and an occasional vacation. Sometimes it is fun going to a new place, especially on vacation. But, one fact always remains true: There's nothing like being at home. I love to get away, but even more, I love returning to home!

Our oldest son just came home for the holidays after his first semester at college. He loves his classes, friends, campus food, and school life—but for him, there's nothing like being at home. Nothing is as good as home-cooked meals or a comfortable-sized room instead of a dorm room shared with a college bud. Nothing tops the relational bonds of family, home-based traditions, a common history, and shared memories. All these things and more make home a meaningful place for our son to come back to.

The new heaven and new earth will be our true home—the ultimate and perpetual place of peace, rest, and community that all of us long for. In Philippians 3:20, Paul reminds us that "our citizenship is in heaven." On earth, we are just strangers passing through. We are ambassadors from a land we've not gone to, yet somehow we long for it as our true home.

If we can experience the concept of home in an imperfect world and an imperfect family, how much more will we feel home in the eternal state? It is there that we will forever experience God's presence and complete relational unity, joy, peace, rest, and fulfillment.

As Revelation 21:4 says, "There will be no more death or mourning or crying or pain, for the old order of things has passed away." We will finally be home in the truest sense of the concept. For those of us who know the Lord, it is our guaranteed and permanent destiny because of what Christ accomplished for us on the cross almost 2,000 years ago.

Thirsty?

In John chapter 4, we read a critically important and relatable story about the woman at the well. John records the moment when Jesus asks her for a drink of water, which sparked a conversation about the thirst within the woman's soul. In a direct but loving way, Jesus heightened the tension by pointing out the ways in which the woman had been unsuc-cessfully trying to quench her spiritual thirst. She had been married several times and at this time was shacked up with a new boyfriend. She had been following a pattern of tempo-rarily quenching her thirst—clinging to any-thing or anyone who promised to make her life feel complete.

Using the well as an object lesson, Jesus told her, "Everyone who drinks this water will be thirsty again, but whoever drinks the water I give them will never thirst. Indeed, the water I give them will become in them a spring of water welling up to eternal life" (verses 13-14). As a result of Jesus's direct but loving conversation, the woman's thirst was finally quenched in a fulfilling way, and she couldn't help but tell others about what Jesus had done in her life.

Here in Revelation 21, John—the same author who documented the story of the woman at the well—recorded these powerful words of Jesus: "It is done. I am the Alpha and the Omega, the Beginning and the End. To the thirsty I will give water without cost from the spring of the water of life" (verse 6).

Alpha and *omega* are the first and last let-ters in the Greek alphabet. Jesus is God from A to Z and everything in between. He knows how to quench our spiri-tual thirst. You've probably heard it said that every person has a God-shaped void in their soul. Only God can fill it, and until he does, people try in vain to quench their thirst with all sorts of things. But nothing this world offers can ever fully and finally satisfy. Only Jesus can.

The world is littered with story after story of lives that were cut short because of destructive habits, patterns, addictions, and hopeless endeavors—all in attempts to fill the void within. Those who dwell in the eternal state will never thirst again and will know permanent satisfaction. They will not have even a hint of longing, dissatisfaction, want, or emptiness.

How about you? Do you still thirst? Do you know the thirst-quencher? If not, you can ask him to once and for all quench your thirst right now. Jesus's offer doesn't apply only to the woman at the well. In John 7:37, he made this simple yet bold statement: "Let anyone who is thirsty come to me and drink." *Anyone.* That includes you. If you are not sure whether you have a relationship with Christ, please read the next and final chapter. Jesus's last words in the Bible are powerful, sobering, and full of hope if we heed them. Let's take a look!

CHAPTER 17

Nearer Than We Think

Look, I am coming soon! My reward is with me, and I will give to each person according to what they have done. I am the Alpha and the Omega, the First and the Last, the Beginning and the End.

REVELATION 22:12-13

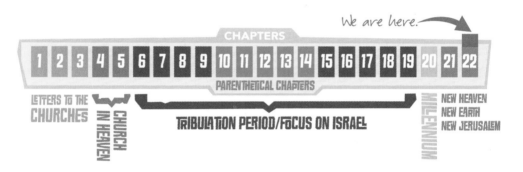

We are here.

CHAPTERS

1 2 3 4 5 6 7 8 9 10 11 12 13 14 15 16 17 18 19 20 21 22

PARENTHETICAL CHAPTERS

LETTERS TO THE CHURCHES | CHURCH IN HEAVEN | TRIBULATION PERIOD/FOCUS ON ISRAEL | MILLENNIUM | NEW HEAVEN NEW EARTH NEW JERUSALEM

When my first child was born, I started a birthday journal for him. Each year on his birthday I would record an entry. I've continued this tradition with my other children as well. Each year on their birthdays I write a few pages citing any key milestones since their last birthday. I recount funny stories, encourage them about their character and spiritual growth, and share a Bible verse or spiritual truth that I sense the Lord is leading me to record for them.

I remember penning the first entry and how my eldest child's eighteenth birthday seemed like an eternity away. Well, my son is 18 and just finished his first semester at college. I gave the book to him as part of his high school graduation gift—8 months ago! A milestone that seemed like it would take forever to

JOURNAL

1/3RD PROPHECY

80% FULFILLED

20% STILL FUTURE

2500+ PROPHECIES

There are approximately 2,500 prophecies in the Bible, 80 percent of which (or 2,000) have been fulfilled to the letter with no errors. The remaining 500 or so prophecies are yet to be fulfilled. [1]

arrive has come and gone, and I'm less than a year away from giving the birthday journal for my second child, a daughter, on her eighteenth birthday! Milestones that seem so far away somehow sneak up on you before you know it.

The events described in Revelation edge closer to us with each passing day. Though almost 2,000 years have passed since John wrote his words, God is always right on schedule. The end-time events foretold in Scripture are not mere mythology. Revelation is not a fictitious book of literary fantasy or a deceptive religious text designed to scare us into obedience. The events described in Revelation will literally come true one day relatively soon. The hundreds of fulfilled prophecies in Scripture serve as a major proof and warning that all the events prophesied to take place in the future will one day come to pass.

How Soon Is Soon?

John was assured by an angel in Revelation 22:6 that "these words are trustworthy and true." As John reflected on the visions he had and the words he penned, he must have had to pinch himself at times to make sure it was all real. Then the angel went on to say that all the things described in Revelation "must soon take place." But that was nearly 2,000 years ago! What did the angel mean by soon?

We need to keep in mind that the things John was told would "soon take place" also include the sequential church periods—prophetically described in chapters 2–3 of Revelation. Technically, and literally, the beginning of all the events in Revelation began when John penned the message from the angel. John was part of the first period of church history, prophetically described as the church in Ephesus. The other church history periods would follow, then the rapture, then the beginning of the tribulation period. After the tribulation comes the 1,000-year millennial kingdom, then the eternal state.

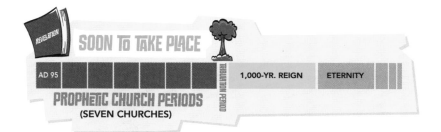

This means the eternal state is at least 1,007+ years away at the moment you are reading this. Obviously the angel wasn't saying everything in Revelation would *soon* take place. Rather, he was reminding John (and us) that the sequence of events described in Revelation 2–22 were about to begin in John's day.

The angel was letting John know that this last chapter of Revelation brought things to a conclusion. This was to be the final Holy Spirit-inspired message to John, and immediately following would be the church age (of which John was already in the first period) that would ultimately lead up to the tribulation period, the millennial kingdom, and the eternal state. There would be no additional ages or dispensations in between the completion of the writing of Revelation and the chronological list of events described therein. God's last-days plan was already in full swing! From the book of Hebrews we understand that the apostles who were still writing Scripture were already in the last days.

> Hebrews 1:1-2—In the past God spoke to our ancestors through the prophets at many times and in various ways, but in these last days he has spoken to us by his Son, whom he appointed heir of all things, and through whom also he made the universe.

I believe the angel was also indicating that the end-time events in particular would occur rapidly in tachometer-like birth pains. Back in chapter 2, we learned about the Greek word *tachos*. It forms the base of the word *tachometer* and has to do with the rapidity of associated events. Throughout Revelation, particularly in the first and last chapters, the word is used and is translated as "soon." Relative to eternity, any future event could be considered to take place soon, but part of what John was conveying in the opening and closing chapters of Revelation is a little different in nature. What we should keep in mind is that once everything is in place, all the end-time events related to Jesus's return will happen rapidly at tachometer-like speed.

As one Bible prophecy teacher says, these end-time events will occur at a time when the signs and conditions are revved up. This matches Jesus's description of the end-time signs as birth pains that will become more intense and frequent as time moves forward. These birth pains will rev things up and lead to the primary *tachos* event. Once the first key revolution occurs—the rapture of the church—the ensuing details described in Revelation will happen in rapid succession. Once the dominoes begin to fall, they will fall quickly until it comes time to usher in the return of Christ to set up his earthly kingdom!

Unsealed Truth Revisited

Also, if you'll recall from our study of Revelation chapter 1, we discussed how the Old Testament prophet Daniel was told that his prophecies would be sealed up until the time of the end. Here, in Revelation 22, we see the opposite command given in the closing chapter of the Bible. In verse 10, the angel told John, "Do not seal up the words of the prophecy of this scroll, because the time is near."

Though it would take some time for all the various New Testament letters circulating through the churches to eventually become canonized (officially placed into the collection of inspired documents we now call the Bible), the Holy Spirit—the true author of Scripture (2 Peter 1:21)—knew that when John penned this final chapter of Revelation the Bible would be complete. All that the church would ever need to know during this age of grace had now been fully unsealed. Perhaps not fully understood, but all the information God needed to transmit to his people was now in place.

The Holy Spirit also knew that as history inched closer to the time of the end, unsealed prophetic truth would become clearer to the godly men and women who would study it. The early church held to a literal interpretation of end-time prophecies, but from around AD 313–600 the church became so intertwined with the state (Rome) that pagan practices muddied the teachings of Scripture—particularly eschatology, which began to be interpreted in allegorical ways. Then from about AD 600–1517, during the Dark Ages, Bibles were chained to priests' pulpits and kept from the masses. As a result, prophetic understanding was all but lost except to a small remnant. After the Reformation, however, when it was permissible for people to read Scripture for themselves (and it became available in their own languages), a revived understanding of end-time prophecies slowly emerged.

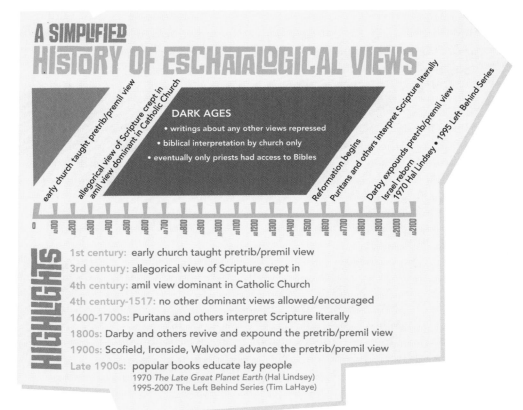

A SIMPLIFIED HISTORY OF ESCHATOLOGICAL VIEWS

- early church taught pretrib/premil view
- allegorical view of Scripture crept in
- amil view dominant in Catholic Church

DARK AGES
- writings about any other views repressed
- biblical interpretation by church only
- eventually only priests had access to Bibles

Reformation begins
Puritans and others interpret Scripture literally
Darby expounds pretrib/premil view
Israel reborn
1970 Hal Lindsey • 1995 Left Behind Series

0 100 200 300 400 500 600 700 800 900 1000 1100 1200 1300 1400 1500 1600 1700 1800 1900 2000 2100

HIGHLIGHTS

1st century: early church taught pretrib/premil view
3rd century: allegorical view of Scripture crept in
4th century: amil view dominant in Catholic Church
4th century-1517: no other dominant views allowed/encouraged
1600-1700s: Puritans and others interpret Scripture literally
1800s: Darby and others revive and expound the pretrib/premil view
1900s: Scofield, Ironside, Walvoord advance the pretrib/premil view
Late 1900s: popular books educate lay people
1970 *The Late Great Planet Earth* (Hal Lindsey)
1995-2007 *The Left Behind Series* (Tim LaHaye)

During the 1600s, larger groups of believers—including the Puritans and some others—returned to the early church's method of interpreting end-time prophecies literally. This led to a revived belief that Israel would literally become a nation again. This belief continued to grow during the 1700s and 1800s and was taught systematically by dispensational teachers and other theologians. The notion that Israel would become a nation again seemed like absolute insanity to most—yet the prophecy was clearly and literally fulfilled in 1948!

The Power of Last Words

As we learned at the beginning of this book, the word *apocalypse* simply means "unveiling" and is taken from the first verse of Revelation, which literally reads, "The unveiling of the Messiah Jesus Christ." As would be fitting for the final chapter of the final book of Scripture, the now fully unveiled Jesus shared some powerful closing words for the billions of people who would live during the church age.

In Revelation 22:12-20, Jesus suddenly breaks into the narrative. At the conclusion of the angel's instructions to John about not sealing up the prophecies of Revelation, the next words are those of Jesus. We don't know if Jesus broke in at that moment, or if John took some time to pray about how to conclude the book before receiving these words from the Lord, but in any case, there is no setup—just bold, final, powerful words from the Lord Jesus. These are his last recorded in Scripture, so obviously they carry tremendous weight. At times it is difficult to separate which comments are John's and which are directly from Jesus, but either way, Jesus affirms the truth being shared in this critical last chapter of the Bible.

A Final Invitation

In Jesus's closing words to the churches we find an invitation and a warning. True to character, Jesus first offers grace. Nearly 2,000 years ago, he left heaven to enter a fallen world as a helpless baby, grew to manhood experiencing every temptation you and I could ever face, lived a sinless life as the spotless Lamb, then sacrificed himself to offer salvation to everyone who would accept the amazing gift. Here again in the final words of Scripture, Jesus offers grace— one last time.

In Revelation 22:12-17 we read,

> Look, I am coming soon! My reward is with me, and I will give to each person according to what they have done. I am the Alpha and the Omega, the First and the Last, the Beginning and the End. Blessed are those who wash their robes, that they may have the right to the tree of life and may go through the gates into the city. Outside are the dogs, those who practice magic arts, the sexually immoral, the murderers, the idolaters and everyone who loves and practices falsehood. I, Jesus, have sent my angel to give you this testimony for the churches. I am the Root and the Offspring of David, and the bright Morning Star. The Spirit and the bride say, "Come!" And let the one who hears say, "Come!" Let the one who is thirsty come; and let the one who wishes take the free gift of the water of life.

This passage is pregnant with grace, mercy, love, and awe. It also has some hints of judgment. In our modern era in which seemingly anything goes— a time when things historically seen as destructive to people and society are now accepted and celebrated and where words like *sin* and *unrighteous* are condemned as politically incorrect relics from a stuffy bygone era—God still has standards. In a world where change is constant, God remains the same. He does not shift his positions to fit cultural sensibilities (Hebrews 13:8; James 1:17).

Within this grace-filled passage Christ also mentions those who violate his standard by their willful practice. Conviction—a sense of wrongdoing—is needed before people can receive the grace and forgiveness so freely offered by Jesus. Both grace and forgiveness are necessary components to God's redemptive plan. You cannot have one without the other.

At the end of the previous chapter I shared about how Jesus quenched the thirst of the woman at the well, and how he satisfies the thirst of all who come to him. We find this metaphor about spiritual thirst again in Revelation 22:17, where we read this simple yet profound invitation: "Let the one who is thirsty come; and let the one who wishes take the free gift of the water of life." It doesn't get any clearer than that! God has done everything possible to reconcile mankind to himself. But God is gracious and will not force people to accept this gift or seek it out.

A Final Warning

At the same time Jesus gives a final invitation to be reconciled to God, he also proclaims a final warning regarding the sacredness of Scripture. While this warning relates primarily to the words of Revelation, I believe we can also apply it to all of Scripture. We know from 2 Timothy 3:16 and 2 Peter 1:21 that the 66 books of the Bible were inspired (God-breathed) by the Holy Spirit, and many Bible teachers believe God sovereignly placed these books into the canon of Scripture. If God can create the universe by simply speaking it into existence, then surely he is able to coordinate the gathering of inspired texts into a single collection. These 66 books are not a random assortment of writings that merely happened to get lumped together. They were sovereignly placed together and are intricately interwoven, without error (in their original manuscripts), and have been preserved through the ages for all mankind to read, hear, and understand.

With that said, let's look at what Jesus said about Revelation—the concluding book of God's 66-book love letter to us. He said in Revelation 22:18-20,

> I warn everyone who hears the words of the prophecy of this scroll: If anyone adds anything to them, God will add to that person the plagues described in this scroll. And if anyone takes words away from this scroll of prophecy, God will take away from that person any share in the tree of life and in the Holy City, which are described in this scroll. He who testifies to these things says, "Yes, I am coming soon."

Many religious cults use the Bible as a source of truth, but they also add to it or take away from it. They use the Bible plus another book or authority. Typically they will use the Bible plus the words of their own so-called prophets, vicars (supposed representatives of Christ), or founders. *Adding to* or *taking away from Scripture* is a key feature of any cult.

Try as they might, cults can't morph God's Word to fit their agenda, and neither can we force Scripture to accommodate our own purposes. We can either accept the plain truth of God's Word as the final authority, or not. Such acceptance doesn't require that we fully understand the Bible or that we have it all figured out. But I can honestly say that during the 35-plus years I have walked with the Lord, any question I have ever had about Scripture has been adequately answered and has further convinced me that the Bible is a supernatural book. In some cases that means I accept that I won't have all the answers until I see God face to face, but the patterns of evidence show that every nuance of Scripture is ordained by God.

Final Thoughts

At the conclusion of the Savior's final words, John chimes in to affirm them. In Revelation 22:20, John wrote, "Amen. Come, Lord Jesus." Then in verse 21, John signed off with these words: "The grace of the Lord Jesus be with God's people. Amen."

As time goes on, I find myself torn like the apostle Paul, who wanted to depart and be with the Lord yet realized there was still important ministry to do on Earth. As long as there are people who need to know the Lord, I want to stay here and work for kingdom purposes. I also love watching my family grow and move into new phases of life. I love spending time with my wife. I love serving through a local church. I love my friendships and my hobbies. Even in the midst of a fallen world, my life feels rich.

> Philippians 1:21-23—For to me, to live is Christ and to die is gain. If I am to go on living in the body, this will mean fruitful labor for me. Yet what shall I choose? I do not know! I am torn between the two: I desire to depart and be with Christ, which is better by far.

But at the same time, I see the signs and conditions that Jesus and the apostles said to look for. The world is a dark, scary place if viewed apart from the prophetic lens of Scripture. As believers we know what lies ahead, but the condition of the world is still troubling when living in it in real time. So I long for the Lord to return. There's nothing I want more. There's not a single problem I have that the rapture won't fix.

There is a convergence of events occurring right now that is unlike anything that has happened in the history of this world. You and I live in the most exciting time since the first coming of Christ. If that sounds like a bold statement, it is. But, there is evidence to back it up. In my book *The Non-Prophet's Guide™ to the End Times*, I spent seven full chapters discussing the specific signs that would characterize the era immediately before the return of Christ. I'll just say that between the time I completed that book to now, those signs have all continued to increase in intensity, and there is no evidence of them lessening until the Lord returns.

If you know the Lord but are discouraged, overwhelmed, fearful, or stressed about the conditions of society and the world, look up, for your redemption is close (Luke 21:28)! Consider what you now know about the book of Revelation and compare it to our day. You'll notice remarkable and undeniable similarities between the two as the stage is being set for end-time events to take place.

If you don't know the Lord but somehow hung with me through this book, please receive him now. To be very direct, time is short. Please do not harden your heart toward the truths in the book of Revelation. Make an honest effort to seek answers, and you may be surprised at what you find. If you wish to know more about how to receive Christ, please contact me or read the final two chapters in my book, *The Non-Prophet's Guide™ to the End Times*, where I explain it in detail.

As we consider all the evil, rebellion, abuse, unfairness, and pain in our present day, we need to remember that God is fair and sovereign. Though we live in an era where we don't see God and wickedness continues to proliferate, when the dust settles after the events prophesied in Revelation, everything will have been made right. When all is said and done, no one will question God's goodness, righteousness, fairness, sovereignty, or omnipotence. All will be perfect. We can rest assured of this because it has been revealed to us by the supreme focal point of the book of Revelation and all of Scripture—the Lord Jesus Christ!

Revelation 19:10 —The testimony of Jesus is the spirit of prophecy (NKJV).

NOTES

Chapter 1—One Mega-Story

1. Chuck Missler, "The Book of Revelation," *Koinonia House* (July 1, 1995), http://www.khouse.org/articles/1995/41/.

Chapter 2—The Full Picture of Jesus—Meek and Wild

1. Chuck Missler, "Seven Letters to Seven Churches," *Koinonia House* (January 1, 2018), http://www.khouse.org/articles/2018/1315/.

Chapter 3—Seven Overlooked Letters Written to You

1. "Competing Worldviews Influence Today's Christians" *Barna* (May 9, 2017), https://www.barna.com/research/competing-worldviews-influence-todays-christians/.

Chapter 4—Snatched Away!

1. There is some discussion among Bible scholars as to what the "seven lamps" were. In Hebrews 9:23, we are told that the Old Testament tabernacle—the tent the Israelites used for their worship of God in the wilderness—was a copy "of the heavenly things." Within the tabernacle was a seven-branched candlestick known as a menorah, which may represent the "seven lamps" present in heaven.

2. Chuck Missler, "The Book of Revelation," *Koinonia House* (July 1, 1995), http://www.khouse.org/articles/1995/41/.

Chapter 5—The Tribulation Begins

1. Charles Q. Choi, "Can big earthquakes trigger a domino effect?" *Science on NBC News* (May 25, 2008), http://www.nbcnews.com/id/24820044/ns/technology_and_science-science/t/can-big-earthquakes-trigger-domino-effect/#.WywMDC-ZMW8.

2. Trevor Nace, "Layers of the Earth: What Lies Beneath the Earth's Crust," *Forbes* (January 16, 2016), https://www.forbes.com/sites/trevornace/2016/01/16/layers-of-the-earth-lies-beneath-earths-crust/#64f17931441d.

3. "Billionaire bunkers: How the 1% are preparing for the apocalypse," CNN (October 17, 2017), https://www.cnn.com/style/article/doomsday-luxury-bunkers/index.html.

Chapter 6—Brand of Brothers

1. Adam Eliyahu Berkowitz, "DNA Studies Trace Jewish Priestly Lineage from Biblical Times," *Breaking Israel News* (September 30, 2015), https://www.breakingisraelnews.com/49932/dna-studies-prove-existence-of-biblical-priestly-class-health-and-science/.

Chapter 7—The Paranormal Becomes the New Normal

1. Robert Bridge, "10 mind-blowing facts about the CERN Large Collider you need to know," *RT Question More* (August 31, 2015), https://www.rt.com/op-ed/313922-cern-collider-hadron-higgs/.

2. "Current World Population," *Worldometers*, https://www.worldometers.info/world-population/.

3. Rebecca Flood, "China unveils gene technology to create SUPERHUMANS with hyper-muscular test-tube dogs," *Express* (July 18, 2017), https://www.express.co.uk/news/world/828981/China-genetic-engineering-super-soldiers-dogs; Dan Falvey, "Top secret HUMAN TESTING in China to create SUPERHUMAN army in military revamp," *Express* (January 24, 2018), https://www.express.co.uk/news/world/909023/china-military-power-superhuman-army-science-testing-secret-plot-world-war-3-trump-us.

4. Sarwant Singh, "Transhuman and the Future of Humanity: 7 Ways the World Will Change by 2030," *Forbes* (November 20, 2017), https://www.forbes.com/sites/sarwantsingh/2017/11/20/transhumanism-and -the-future-of-humanity-seven-ways-the-world-will-change-by-2030/#33df12f57d79.

5. Kelsey D. Atherton, "Marines Are Testing a Robot Dog for War," *Popular Science* (September 22, 2015), https://www.popsci.com/marines-test-robot-dog-for-war; Will Nicol, "9 Military Robots that Are Totally Terrifying…and Oddly Adorable," *Digital Trends* (March 4, 2017), https://www.digitaltrends.com/cool- tech/coolest-military-robots/; Larry Greenemeier, "Bots of Burden: U.S. Army Recruiting an Array of Animal-Inspired Robots to Assist Battlefield Troops, *Scientific American* (March 29, 2012), https://www .scientificamerican.com/article/animal-inspired-robots/.

Chapter 9—The Tipping Point

1. Christopher Klein, "The Birth of Satellite TV, 50 Years Ago," *History* (July 23, 2012), https://www.history .com/news/the-birth-of-satellite-tv-50-years-ago; "CNN," *Encyclopaedia Britannica* (last updated March 6, 2019), https://www.britannica.com/topic/Cable-News-Network; Steven Tweedle, "The world's first smart- phone, Simon, was created 15 years before the iPhone," *Business Insider* (June 14, 2015), https://www.busi nessinsider.com/worlds-first-smartphone-simon-launched-before-iphone-2015-6; Simon Hill, "From J-Phone to Lumia 1020: A complete history of the camera phone" (August 11, 2013), https://www.digi taltrends.com/mobile/camera-phone-history/; Alice Truong, "It's official: Meerkat has lost the live-stream- ing battle to Periscope," *Quartz* (March 5, 2016), https://qz.com/632017/its-official-meerkat-has-lost-the -live-streaming-battle-to-periscope/; Michelle Castillo, "Mark Zuckerberg puts employees on 'lockdown' for two months to launch Facebook Live; Report," CNBC (March 6, 2017), https://www.cnbc.com/2017/03/06/ zuckerberg-put-employees-on-lockdown-to-launch-facebook-live-wsj.html.

Chapter 10—Mega-Signs of an Epic Story

1. Cristina Maza, "Christian Persecution and Genocide Is Worse Now Than 'Any Time in History,' Report Says," *Newsweek* (January 4, 2018), https://www.newsweek.com/christian-persecution-genocide-worse -ever-770462, https://www.washingtonpost.com/news/worldviews/wp/2018/04/11/resurgent-traditional -antisemitism-behind-corrosion-of-jewish-life-report-warns/?noredirect=on&utm_term=.9b72468a3d74).

Chapter 11—The Unholy Fake Trinity

1. The editors of *Encyclopaedia Britannica*, "Titus," *Encyclopaedia Britannica* (January 25, 2019), https://www .britannica.com/biography/Titus.

Chapter 12—Three Earth-Circling Angels and Seven Angry Bowls

1. The editors of *Encyclopaedia Britannica*, "Zion," *Encyclopaedia Britannica*, https://www.britannica.com/ place/Zion-hill-Jerusalem.

Chapter 13—The End of Babylon's Babbling

1. "The Facts," *Polaris*, https://polarisproject.org/human-trafficking/facts.

Chapter 17—Nearer Than We Think

1. See www.reasons.org/explore/blogs/todays-new-reason-to-believe/read/tnrtb/2003/08/22/fulfilled-prophe cy-evidence-for-the-reliability-of-the-Bible.

THE NON-PROPHET'S GUIDE™ TO THE END TIMES

Do you struggle with understanding all the prophecies about the last days? Does it feel like words such as *rapture* and *apocalypse* fly right over your head? You're not alone. It's common to dismiss these and other topics related to Bible prophecy as irrelevant and…well…too complicated.

But *The Non-Prophet's Guide™ to the End Times* changes all that! Prepare to be blessed in an entertaining and meaningful way as this book combines engaging illustrations and down-to-earth explanations to help you navigate the ins and outs of Bible prophecy. There's no better time to grasp God's plan for the future—and for you—than this very moment.

To learn more about Harvest House books and
to read sample chapters, visit our website:

www.harvesthousepublishers.com

HARVEST HOUSE PUBLISHERS
EUGENE, OREGON